5-13-80

Anatomy of Horror:

The Masters
of Occult Fiction

Anatomy of Horror:

The Masters
of Occult Fiction

Glen St John Barclay

St. Martin's Press   New York

Contents

1 *The Lure of the Occult*

In many ways, the most mysterious thing about novels of the occult is that there are not more of them. If one understands the term 'occult' to refer to all kinds of phenomena which appear not to be subject to the laws of the physical universe, the opportunities for the storyteller seem to be limitless.[1] Apart from the fact that he can introduce beings which are not limited to merely human capacities but can do literally anything that he wants them to, the author would seem to be under no obligation to make the events or scenes he describes convincing or even authentic. Nor need he be too concerned with characterization: there is really no point in bothering to analyze the motivations of a vampire for example, since vampires do not exist, and since the only motivation attributed to them even in myth is in fact extreme thirst. It is of course possible for the writer of occult fiction to achieve useful effects by enumerating what might seem to be corroborative details, but these are in practice far more impressive when totally imaginary than when extracted from genuine legends, the details of which are often uninteresting and almost always in dispute.[2] But the attraction of the occult for the writer of limited ability is not due solely to the fact that it makes so few demands on his industry or his talent. Far more important is the fact that it possesses almost infallible popular appeal.

Various esoteric reasons have been put forward from time to time to explain the continuing popularity of the genre. Peter Penzoldt, for example, refers to Freud's argument that the fear of the supernatural, which he thinks provides the raison d'être for the story of the occult, is based on 'the survival of the ancient animistic beliefs such as the faith in the omnipotence of thought and in instantaneous wish fulfilments.' Penzoldt accordingly concludes that the role of the occult story is to combat a 'secret and persistent faith in the unknown', and that individuals require to be assured continually that 'the horrors we have been contemplating are naught but fiction', precisely at those times when they are most prone to insist upon their own rationality. Howard P. Lovecraft expressed much the same idea in radically different language, when he claimed:

> the oldest and strongest emotion of mankind is fear
> . . . men with minds sensitive to hereditary impulse
> will always tremble at the thought of the hidden and
> fathomless worlds of strange life which may pulsate in
> the gulfs beyond the stars, or press hideously upon our
> own globe in unholy dimensions which only the dead
> and the moonstruck can glimpse.[3]

There are simpler explanations, quite apart from the fact that Lovecraft's, at least, is totally dishonest. Lovecraft by his own account never believed in his own inventions of strange life beyond the stars, and as an atheist and a materialist certainly never believed that the dead could glimpse anything. The only unholy dimensions pressing upon our own globe of which Lovecraft was ever aware, were those of human existence itself, most aspects and representatives of which he loathed beyond measure. But the fact is that the inherent appeal of the story of the occult lies in its capacity not to exorcize faith in the unknown, but to reinforce it. Any story which in any sense refers to the intervention of the supernatural in human affairs necessarily affirms that the supernatural exists. It holds out the reality of alternative modes and realms of existence beyond the physical limitations of our material life. In doing so, it responds directly to what is certainly man's most abiding concern, the prospect of his own personal annihilation and oblivion in death. The aspect of supernatural fear is, by comparison, of very little relevance indeed. One may be frightened at the prospect of seeing a ghost oneself, through fear of what the effect of such a vision might be upon one's own nerves; but one is always immensely interested and reassured to hear that someone else has had such an experience, since a ghost is *de facto* proof of personal immortality, in however unsatisfactory a form. In any case, it is literally impossible to contemplate any horrors from beyond the grave worse than those which one might encounter at the hands of the living. Anybody given a choice between being assaulted and murdered by a psychopathic street gang, and having an encounter with Dracula, would choose Dracula every time, partly because Dracula can always be repelled by simple defences such as holy water and the sign of the cross, which are notoriously ineffective against human monsters, and also because the unequivocal apparition of a supernatural being would be the most convincing proof possible of one's own possession of a supernatural existence.

Nor does it seem actually true that people turn to occult fiction as a means of reinforcing their confidence in their own rationality. It is obviously impossible to prove statistically any kind of correlation between the popularity of occult stories and the incidence of religious belief. Occult fiction has always been read, and it has been read most avidly when it has been written by authors of unusual technical skill, regardless of whether the churches have been full or empty at the time. It is certainly probable that the popularity of occult fiction has never been greater, nor the authority of conventional religion less, than at this present stage in human history; but this situation would seem to support a quite different argument. It would have been difficult in the past for a believer in orthodox Christianity to sustain any kind of serious interest in the occult with a clear conscience, because of the unanimous opposition of the clergy to anybody other than themselves having any dealings with such matters. At the same time, contemporary experience shows clearly that a decline in the authority of orthodox religion is not necessarily accompanied by a decline of faith or hope in the unknown. Exactly the opposite would in fact seem to be the case: individuals turn to the occult in such circumstances with vastly enhanced interest, partly because the conventional prohibitions no longer deter them, but also because of their concern to find reassurances of personal survival which the churches are no longer able to provide convincingly. Moreover, the decline in respect for conventional theology in contemporary times has been accompanied by a decline in respect for conventional science. The clergy have not suffered at the hands of the scientists: they have suffered together at the hands of the parapsychologists. The work of Carl Jung, Arthur Koestler, the Rhines, E. Y. Evans-Wentz, Raymond L. Moody and literally scores of others has helped to create a contemporary mood in which it is positively conventional to accept as a working hypothesis the existence of alternative levels of existence and the occasional practical irrelevance of space and time.[4] In such a climate, the story of the occult becomes positively a potential work of social realism.

The story of the occult has still other grounds of appeal, no less effective for being less respectable. In times when censorship or conventions operated to deter authors from dealing specifically with certain human situations, the occult provided a reservoir of images which could be used to convey symbolically what could not be presented literally. Lesbianism, the physical experience of the orgasm and oral sex in particular could be depicted and their emotional intensity conveyed only under the guise of parables about vampires and ladies, composed by authors who may not always have fully admitted to themselves what they were actually doing. Similarly, Lovecraft's hatred for the vast majority of his fellow-beings, and his revulsion from most of the physical aspects of human life, could be externalized in his visions of slimy and inchoate horrors descending from outer space, or jeering ghouls surfacing in Boston graveyards. Even in less inhibited times, the paraphernalia of certain aspects of the occult provided opportunities to develop fantasies of the physical abuse of women in the pages of ostensibly respectable fiction. Vampirism of course necessarily involved oral assaults on male or female victims by male or female vampires, and the consequent impalement of female vampires by the victims' vengeful relatives. Male vampires, as a point of interest, are customarily beheaded. The ceremony of satanism similarly involved the stripping and physical degradation of women. There are however limits to the extent to which this particular aspect can be developed, simply because there are limits to the number of sadistically interesting things that can be done to the human body: when William P. Blatty describes his heroine masturbating with a crucifix in *The Exorcist*, one feels that the end of the road might in fact have been reached.

There is another reason for the appeal of the occult, however, the limits of which can never be reached. This is the simple fact that for many people occult experiences form an intrinsic part of human existence, and therefore need to be taken account of in any systematic study of human life. This attitude seems to have been shared by so many writers of undoubted importance that a comprehensive study of the occult in fiction would come very close indeed to being a history of world literature. The occult element emerges even in authors who represent themselves as atheists or agnostics, and deny the presence of any supernatural element in their writings. Thus for example, George Eliot, the author of arguably the greatest English novel of the nineteenth century, and a self-professed realist, who defined realism as 'the doctrine that all truth and beauty are to be attained by a humble and faithful study of nature, and not by substituting vague forms, bred by imagination on the mists of feeling, in place of definite, substantial reality', introduces in *Adam Bede* an episode in which the village carpenter's son hears a sound which brings to his mind the image of a willow wand striking the door of his house. He later finds the drowned body of his father, wedged against a willow tree growing in a brook some distance away. George Eliot does indeed refer to a village superstition that forewarnings of death may be conveyed in this way, but there is no way in which Adam Bede's experience can be interpreted other than as validating the superstition: it is presented as a simple fact of life, which can be nothing other than a precognitive intimation of death.

George Eliot was indeed no writer of ghost stories. Henry James was; but he was also the most self-conscious of literary artists, who made an explicit distinction between his ghost stories and his stories of social realism. It is in one of the latter, *The Portrait of a Lady*, that he describes one of the most frequently reported of occult occurrences, the appearance of the phantasm of the dead to a close friend. Again, there is no possible suggestion of any possible error or hallucination. Indeed, James makes it clear that neither of the two persons involved had any particular belief in the possibility of the survival of the human personality after death: Isabel Archer, the woman who sees the apparition, had been looking forward to death as a release from thought and feeling; and

Ralph Touchett, the man who dies, had merely reflected that it was 'all over' with himself. Nor is there any possibility that James, any more than George Eliot, was introducing a mild thrill into his novel to enhance its popularity: nobody who had already persevered to this stage of *The Portrait of a Lady* could possibly be interested in even the mildest of literary thrills. The only possible assumption is that both Henry James and George Eliot believed that such experiences did in fact occur in real life, or at least believed that their readers thought they did.

The most peculiar example of an author who seems to have introduced occult elements into his stories positively against his will is Joseph Conrad, who was even more committed to the ideal of self-conscious literary artistry than Henry James, if that were possible. Nobody could ever believe that Conrad wrote a line for any purpose other than to gratify his own artistic ideals. He also insisted throughout his life on maintaining an unyielding agnosticism, confronting the prospect of death with a total rejection of hope or consolation. Yet Conrad wrote two stories, one of them at least partly autobiographical, in which occult interventions are fundamental to the development of the plot. He did so despite the fact that he insisted in his prefaces to the stories that they were in fact not about the supernatural. He even expressed surprise that more than one critic had been inclined to imagine that *The Shadow Line* was

> intended to touch on the supernatural.... But as a matter of fact my imagination is not made of stuff so elastic as all that.... Whatever my native modesty may be it will never condescend so low as to seek help for my imagination within those vain imaginings common to all ages and that in themselves are enough to fill all lovers of mankind with unutterable sadness ... there is nothing supernatural in it.

This is explicit enough. However, it does not alter the fact that *The Shadow Line* is really all about the supernatural. A young officer is appointed skipper of a sailing-ship, following the death of the former captain, a 'stern, grim, wind-tanned, rough, sea-salted, taciturn sailor of sixty-five', who, according to the admittedly fever-stricken mate, had expressed before he died the wish that the ship and its crew would never make port. When the ship unexpectedly runs into a patch of dead calm, about the place where the former captain died, the mate explains that 'it was the fault of the "old man" – the late captain – ambushed down there under the sea with some evil intention'. The calm continues. 'Mysterious currents' drift the ship off course. The new skipper remarks that 'It's like being bewitched, upon my word.' The crew are stricken with fever as well. The wind behaves completely unpredictably: 'just about sunrise we got for an hour an inexplicable, steady breeze, right in our teeth. There was no sense in it. It fitted neither with the season of the year, nor with the secular experience of seamen as recorded in books, nor with the aspect of the sky. Only purposeful malevolence could account for it.' The ship is then battered by an equally unnatural storm, at a time when neither the crew nor the rigging are capable of coping with any new emergency. At this stage the mate appears on deck and challenges the spirit of the dead captain with 'such a loud laugh as I had never heard before. It was a provoking, mocking peal, with a hair-raising, screeching over-note of defiance.' Almost immediately, the wind freshens for the first time in seventeen days, blows 'true, true to a hair', and carries the ship and its crew safely to port. The evil spell has been exorcized.

There is no question but that *The Shadow Line* is presented as a story of the occult, the events of which do not permit natural explanation. Conrad no doubt had his own reasons for pretending otherwise. It was not that he did not know what a story of the occult was: another story of his, *The Inn of the Two Witches*, depends upon the credibility of a warning from beyond the grave. An English naval officer and his coxswain land on the coast of Spain during the Peninsular War. The officer goes back to the ship, leaving the coxswain to go ahead on his own to a rendezvous with a Spanish guerrilla leader. Returning later to the village where they had landed, the officer puts up for the night at an inn. After locking the door of his room, the officer hears 'the blood beating in his ears with a confused rushing noise, in which there seemed to be a voice uttering the words: "Mr Byrne, look out, sir!"' He again hears his coxswain's voice 'speaking earnestly somewhere near'. Later, Byrne finds the body of his coxswain in a cupboard. He puts the body on the bed, covers it with a sheet, and resigns himself to sitting up all night, on guard, in a chair. He then sees the baldaquin over the bed 'coming down in short smooth rushes till lowered half way or more, when it took a run and settled swiftly its turtle-back shape with the deep border piece fitting exactly the edge of the bedstead'. This was how the coxswain had died, and the way that he would have died himself, had he not been forewarned by the dead man's spirit. Conrad at least does not try to pretend that this is not a tale of the supernatural. He never refers to it.

There are even more impressive examples of classic authors who have chosen to introduce occult elements into stories presented as works of social realism or at least social commentary. Charles Dickens, like Henry James, wrote stories which were explicitly tales of the supernatural. However, like James, he made a clear distinction between such efforts and his major studies of contemporary urban life. Nonetheless, he introduces into *Our Mutual Friend* the episodes of Mrs Boffin's finding the house full of the faces of its dead owner and his supposedly lost son, and Lizzie Hexham's precognitive intimation of her father's death by drowning. He also began what would unquestionably have been the greatest novel ever written concerned primarily with the intrusion of occult forces in everyday life, if not perhaps with intrusions from beyond the grave: *The Mystery of Edwin Drood*. This novel is presented unequivocally as a psychic duel between two people possessed by paranormal powers. John Jasper, Edwin Drood's uncle and the ultimate wicked uncle of fiction, possesses hypnotic powers which operate unaffected by distance or time, and virtually approximate to telekinesis. Edwin's fiancée, Rosa Budd, with whom he is infatuated, is terrified by him: she tells the other protagonist in the psychic duel, Helena Landless: 'He haunts my thoughts, like a dreadful ghost. I feel that I am never safe from him. I feel as if he could pass in through the wall when he is spoken of.' There is no indication that Dickens meant Rosa's words to be taken literally, but he does make it clear that Jasper is at least able to make Rosa aware of his personality and intentions through particular notes of music, even when his own voice cannot be discerned. He can certainly exert his will over other human beings from a distance, as is seen in the robot-like behaviour of the men who intercept Helena's brother, Neville Landless, outside *The Tilted Waggon*. He may also be able to cast spells upon or somehow affect inanimate objects, as shown by the experience of Canon Chrisparkle, who finds that he has unconsciously wandered to Cloisterham Weir, and that he has 'a strange idea that something unusual hung about the place'. Chrisparkle is unable to see anything unusual by night, but resolves to come back early in the morning, and investigate further. He does so, and promptly notices what he could not have seen at night, Edwin Drood's gold watch and stick-pin, presumably thrown there by Jasper, who has used his psychic powers to have them discovered by Chrisparkle, so that Drood's disappearance will be attributed to murder, and Landless hopefully blamed for it.

His opponent, Helena, is understood to have powers fully capable of matching Jasper's own. She is certainly tele-pathic: as her brother tells Chrisparkle: 'You don't know, sir, yet, what a complete understanding can exist between my sister and me, though no spoken word – per-haps hardly as much as a look – may have passed between us. She not only feels as I have described, but she very well knows that I am taking this opportunity of speaking to you, both for her and for myself.' Chrisparkle has his doubts, but observes on re-entering the house that between Helena and her brother 'an instantaneous recognition passed, in which Mr Chrisparkle saw, or thought he saw, the understanding that had been spoken of, flash out'. This scene is followed by the episode of Rosa's collapse while singing to Jasper's accompaniment, apparently because of the psychic impact of a note which Jasper keeps playing or hinting at in the music. Drood then asks Helena if she would not be afraid of Jasper under similar circumstances, to which she replies: 'Not under any circumstances.' Similarly, when Rosa confesses to Helena her fear that Jasper could pass in through the wall, Helena embraces her so that her 'lustrous gipsy-face drooped over the clinging arms and bosom, and the wild black hair fell down protectingly over the childish form. There was a slumbering gleam of fire in the intense dark eyes, though they were then softened with compassion and admiration. Let whomsoever it most concerned look well to it!' Jasper is obviously to meet his match in the psychic contest. The most probable and certainly the simplest manner in which this would have come about would have been for Helena to confront Jasper after Drood's murder, and extract a full confession from him by exerting her will upon his through hypnosis. The cir-cumstances of the duel would be made more acceptable by the fact that the two adversaries both have associations with the mysterious East: both are described in terms implying Eurasian origins; and Jasper is very clearly acting out the role of a Thug, although Dickens had not yet given any hint as to what element in Jasper's parentage or experiences might account for this obsession. Helena and her brother on the other hand come from Ceylon, and it is suggested that they might have native blood.

There is a melancholy appropriateness in the fact that what might on every account have been the best mystery story of the occult ever written was doomed to remain a mystery forever. It certainly remains the major effort in the genre by a great novelist, although it is not perhaps the major novel in which occult intrusions occur. That distinction undoubtedly belongs to Tolstoy's *Anna Karenina*, whose fundamental plot is in fact the fulfilment of a precognitive dream. In chapter twenty-nine Anna has an intimation of her own death when the train in which she is returning to St Petersburg stops at the station: 'there was a terrible screech and clatter, as though someone were being torn to pieces; then a red light blinded her eyes, and at last a wall rose up and blotted everything out. Anna felt as if she were falling from a height. But all this, far from seeming dreadful, was rather pleasant.' Later in the novel Anna's lover, Count Vronsky, dozes off in a mood in which

memories of the disreputable scenes he had witnessed during the last few days became confused and merged with a mental image of Anna and of a peasant who had played an important part as beater in the bear-hunt.... He awoke in the dark, trembling with horror, and hurriedly lighted a candle. 'What was it? What was the dreadful thing I dreamed? Yes, I know. The peasant-beater – a dirty little man with a matted beard – was stooping down doing something, and of a sudden he began muttering strange words in French.

Yes, there was nothing else in the dream,' he said to himself. 'But why was it so awful?' He vividly recalled the peasant again and the incomprehensible French words the man had uttered and a chill of horror ran down his spine.

He goes to see Anna, without telling her of the dream. She however tells him that she knew that she was going to die and set him free, because she had had a dream about it herself.

> 'Yes, a dream,' she said. 'A dream I had a long time ago. I dreamed that I ran into my bedroom to fetch something or find out something.... And, in the bedroom, in the corner, stood something.... And the something turned around and I saw it was a peasant with a tangled beard, little and dreadful-looking. I wanted to run away, but he stooped down over a sack and was fumbling about in it with his hands.... And all the time he was rummaging, he kept muttering very quickly, in French, you know, rolling his r's: *Il faut le battre, le fer; le broyer, le petrir....*'

The intimations all come together when Anna at last kills herself by throwing herself under the St Petersburg train. 'She tried to get up, to throw herself back; but something huge and relentless struck her on the head and dragged her down on her back. "God forgive me everything!" she murmured, feeling the impossibility of struggling. A little peasant muttering something was working on the rails.' One supposes that the words which the peasant was muttering, the words which Vronsky had not been able to recall when he dreamed of the event and which Anna could not possibly have heard at the actual moment of her death, were the words she had heard in her dream and remembered from it: 'The iron must be beaten, pounded, kneaded....' It is important to note that none of these intimations are presented at all symbolically, as Dickens presents the railroad as an image of death in *Dombey and Son*, in which Carker the manager is in fact killed by a train: as in all the other examples discussed, the occult intrusions in *Anna Karenina* are presented as realities, experienced by real people in real life.

It is perhaps unnecessary to prolong the list. The fact is that many and perhaps most of the major novelists concerned with presenting authentic visions of the human experience, have felt required to include occult intrusions as elements in that experience. On the other hand, it is also true that the occult element is nearly always peripheral or at least unobtrusive. Only Dickens seems to have regarded it as worthwhile to attempt a full-length novel in which the occult was to provide the major element. The reasons are not difficult to imagine. A serious novelist is concerned with human life as it is actually experienced in society; and in any human life lived in the company of other human beings the occult can by definition play only a peripheral and unobtrusive part, if it plays any part at all. The physical universe may indeed be an illusion; but it is an illusion which most of us are compelled to accept as a reality we have to come to terms with for all but a few fleeting moments of our waking lives.

On the other hand, there have been writers who have devoted most or even all of their literary output exclusively to the occult. Most of them have been very bad and very unimportant, and it is reasonable to assume that their chief motivations have been lack of ability to work in any other area of fiction, or the simple desire to make money in the easiest possible way, by cultivating their readers' fears or prurience. But there are still others who by their treatment of occult themes have somehow managed to create or revivify legends, or have themselves become legends in their own lifetimes. They include some of the most popular and certainly most assiduously emulated and plagiarized authors of the past hundred years. They are remarkable phenomena in their own right, and as such they are certainly worth close investigation. They might even have a message for us.

2 *Vampires and Ladies: Sheridan Le Fanu*

It is almost impossible even to think of occult fiction
without thinking of the vampire legend. It should be
equally difficult to think of the vampire legend without
thinking of the man who rediscovered it as a literary
theme in English fiction, and who invested it with the
erotic symbolism which constitutes its sole claim to be
taken seriously in any sense. However, before dealing with
the artist who gave wings to the vampire legend, it is only
polite to spare a word for the legend itself.

Vampirism has provided material for the greater number of stories of the occult which have enjoyed any
literary or popular success, it has inspired probably an
even larger percentage of the films of supernatural terror
produced in the past fifty years, and it kept a number of
British actors and actresses in reasonably permanent employment in the 1950s and 60s. That particular vein
would seem to have been worked out by now, but it must
have made a considerable contribution to the national
economy while its attractions lasted. The nature of the
attraction itself is easy enough to understand. There is
certainly no doubt of its general popularity. In *The
Dracula Myth* Gabriel Ronay lists some twenty-four
recorded varieties of European vampire alone, shadowing
the whole continent from Russia to Ireland. The vam-

pire in fact established itself as a massive and longstanding administrative problem, involving an enormous amount of official and ecclesiastical activity. Ronay deduces that some 30,000 cases of vampirism and associated misdemeanours were investigated officially by the Roman Catholic Church alone from 1520 to the middle of the seventeenth century. Le Fanu himself summarizes the historical background with characteristic style and conviction in *Carmilla*:

> You have heard, no doubt, of the appalling superstition that prevails in Upper and Lower Styria, in Moravia, Silesia, in Turkish Servia, in Poland, even in Russia; the superstition, so we must call it, of the Vampire.
>
> If human testimony, taken with every care and solemnity, judicially presented before commissions innumerable, each consisting of many members, all chosen for integrity and intelligence, and constituting reports more voluminous perhaps than exist upon any one other class of cases, is worth anything, it is difficult to deny, or even to doubt the existence of such a phenomenon as the Vampire.[1]

The argument is compelling as far as it goes. What Le Fanu does fail to mention however is the fact that as a result of all this testimony only one verified case of vampirism was ever detected, and the culprit in this case was a human being who pursued her career as a vampire while still alive, and ceased it immediately after being executed, thereby reversing the essential *modus operandi* of the species.

The claims of the vampire to be treated as a serious historical phenomenon constitute a relatively minor aspect of its attractions for writers of the occult. The sheer oddity of the legend has its own intrinsic interest, quite apart from any possible credibility. The original concept of a blood-sucking demon, 'a psychic sponge', as Professor Wolf calls it, seems to have been first developed by Homer in the *Odyssey*, where, during his visit to the Underworld, Odysseus discovers that the spirits of the dead can acquire the power of speech only by having their vitality restored by what, as spirits, they most conspicuously lack, namely blood. He accordingly provides a pit filled with the blood of sacrificial sheep, to sustain the shade of Tiresias during their conversations. There is nothing very sinister, and certainly nothing erotic about this. There is even a certain logical plausibility, apart from the besetting absurdity that a shade really would have nowhere to put the blood, the lack of which differentiates it from a living person. The whole concept of vampirism does indeed seem to involve quite insuperable problems of hydraulics.

However, there already existed a variation of the myth which did possess unequivocally sinister and erotic aspects, although it was not any the less absurd. Greek folklore had invented a class of demons known as *lamiae*, which the Romans adopted as *striges* or *mormos*, whose practice was to suck the blood of living men, visiting them as either birds of ill-omen or beautiful courtesans. In this latter capacity, the demon apparently made its visitations primarily for purposes of sex, with blood-sucking providing only a minor motivation. The *striges* and *mormos* then became virtually identical with the *succubae*, who had intercourse with men in their dreams. The vampire had thus acquired very early in its evolution two of its most characteristic secondary features, namely, its association with eroticism and its capacity to change its form, especially into that of a creature capable of flight. However, the fundamental concept of the blood-sucking demon seems to have been associated for the next thousand years or so with lycanthropy, because of the tendency of packs of wolves to disinter the bodies of the dead in remoter parts of Europe. This understandably gave rise to the belief that the dead were themselves rising from the grave in the form of wolves to prey upon their fellows and possibly upon the living as well, or alternatively that living human beings might be magically transforming themselves into wolves for this purpose. Thus in Eastern Europe the purely erotic figure of the *succubus* became transformed into the horror of the *cucubuth*, or werewolf, while the Serbs lumped vampires and werewolves together in the single term *vlkoslak*.

The vampire legend acquired its permanent identity as an erotic symbol through its association with a beautiful Transylvanian aristocrat, Countess Elizabeth Bathory, who was born in 1611. Apparently the Countess first became interested in blood as such after she had boxed a maid's ears so hard that blood spurted from the girl's mouth and nose. Some drops fell on the Countess' skin. She gained the impression after wiping them off that the places where the blood had fallen were whiter and smoother than the rest of her skin. The application of human blood thus seemed to have peculiar restorative qualities as a beauty treatment. The idea was the more attractive because of Elizabeth Bathory's inherently sadistic disposition. She had already participated in orgies staged by her cousin, Countess Klara Bathory, a totally dedicated lesbian, who was also addicted to sadism, enlivening her amorous games by flogging servant girls or applying fire to the more sensitive parts of their bodies. Elizabeth herself seems to have remained fundamentally heterosexual. Her interest in torture was primarily directed towards obtaining the greatest possible amount of blood from the bodies of her victims, through lacerations and major surgery. On the other hand, the erotic element was not entirely absent, as she is reported to have experienced orgasms while gyrating naked in her torture chamber, covered in the blood of mutilated and dying peasant girls, whose bodies littered the floor.

The Bathorys seem to have accounted between them for at least 650 young girls from the Transylvanian village of Csejithe, before the authorities at last intervened and ended their careers by execution. Most of the victims seem to have died from the ministrations of Elizabeth, who on a simple count of bodies would thus seem to have been over a hundred times more atrocious than Jack the Ripper. Her impact on local folklore was naturally tremendous. It is thus not surprising that her crimes should have given definite shape to the vampire legend, the consistent ingredients of which have been for the past two hundred years aristocracy, Transylvania, beauty, sadism and sex.

The only quality which the Bathory ladies could not provide was that of the occult. They undoubtedly deserved to be categorized as blood-sucking demons, but they were nonetheless human, and their crimes ended with their deaths. Their impact upon the vampire legend was sustained partly by the fact that the vampire itself provided a thoroughly appropriate and satisfying image for an aristocracy ruthlessly exploiting a supine peasantry, in a style of which the Bathorys were merely extreme examples. Coincidence also served to introduce a new stimulus, just at a time when superstition might have been expected to be losing its force, even in Eastern Europe. About seventy years after the executions of the Bathory cousins, the provinces which they had terrorized were devastated by pestilence in a manner far more wholesale than anything the Bathorys had been able to accomplish. 500,000 people were estimated to have died of smallpox in Transylvania around 1708. Further outbreaks wiped out half the survivors by 1719. The singular horror of the outbreaks naturally encouraged the belief that diabolic agencies were at work. This consideration was seized by the ecclesiastical authorities as an aid to the restoration of their power in territories recently recovered from the Turks; as Gabriel Ronay says, 'a vigorously pursued and dogmatically justified campaign against the widely feared vampires ... afforded a useful lever with which to re-establish the Catholic Church's dominant position and reassert its spiritual influence in the mixed border areas'. The political efficacy of the campaign was hardly impaired by the fact that no vampires were ever actually convicted.

Thus the evolution of the vampire from prototype to completed literary model depends in effect upon a succession of historical accidents, most of them tragic. The concept emerges in Greek thought as a symbol of the alienation of the dead from the living, which can be bridged only by the agency of blood. This naturally gives rise to the notion of the dead seeking blood from the living, in order to establish communication with them, which in turn becomes confused with the idea of demons using the bodies of living men and women in erotic dreams. Fears that the dead might rise from their graves to prey on the living are further excited by the horrible vision of the werewolf, inspired by the actual habits of real animals; the Bathorys provide living examples of beings draining the blood of others for their own pleasure, in a way which both revives the old erotic aspect of the myth and also introduces the element of lesbianism; and outbreaks of disease in the same region, of an intensity to suggest supernatural afflictions, are deliberately used by church authorities to revive belief in the vampire myth. It was also no doubt helpful that the Transylvanian variety of the species was believed to be capable of being destroyed by means which were dramatically acceptable and possessed their own erotic implications. The notion of impalement as a means of eradicating vampires, especially female ones, may well have originated from the activities of the Rumanian monarch, Vlad the Impaler, who may be said to have popularized that custom in the surrounding territories. It was certainly infinitely more satisfactory than the antidotes recommended for other European vampires. The *kathanko* of Crete, for example, could be destroyed only by being boiled in vinegar, which would present insuperable practical as well as dramatic problems, while the *neuntatu* of Saxony was vulnerable only to having a lemon placed in its mouth, which hardly provides a fitting climax to any story. Even worse were the *bruxsa* of Portugal and the *vampiro* of Spain, against which no methods at all were availing. Nobody wants to read a story about a demon which is inevitably going to win because it cannot be defeated.

The vampire began to appear in English literature after 1800, mainly as a poetical symbol of exploitation, or an ill-defined occult threat. It achieved its first real literary significance with the publication of Sheridan Le Fanu's novelette, *Carmilla*, in 1872, the direct forerunner of Bram Stoker's *Dracula*, with which it shares the distinction of being the most famous work of the occult, and the most frequently and shamelessly plagiarized work of fiction of any kind ever written.

Stoker and Le Fanu have little else in common, however. Le Fanu was in the first place a superb literary artist, who died at the very height of his powers: his best story, *The Room at the Dragon Volant*, probably as perfect a piece of narrative as any in English, was published in 1872, the year before his death. He has always been highly acclaimed by practitioners in his own field, if not always by the general public. M. R. James says flatly that Le Fanu 'stands absolutely in the first rank as a writer of ghost stories'. In his very useful introduction to *In a Glass Darkly*, V. S. Pritchett commends his excellence of style, and claims that the short story *Green Tea* is 'among the best half-dozen ghost stories in the English language'.

Nelson Browne says that 'as a literary artist he is the equal of his most brilliant contemporaries'. Dr Penzoldt considers him superior to the Gothic masters, which is faint praise indeed; and Howard P. Lovecraft, whose views on style would admittedly be at the other extreme of the literary spectrum from Le Fanu's, describes him as one of those who carried on the 'romantic, semi-Gothic, quasi-moral tradition ... far down the nineteenth century'.[1] Lovecraft of course has no idea what he is talking about.

Again, unlike Stoker, Le Fanu was undoubtedly inclined by nature to the occult. His temperament is admittedly peculiarly hard to define in other respects. Peter Penzoldt calls him 'always extremely sensitive, and ... probably a neurotic', who towards the end of his life

> became definitely abnormal. He was troubled by horrible nightmares ... he suffered from a severe neurosis ... in the face of neurotic terrors he reacted as a helpless child.... After the death of his wife he retired from the world, living as a recluse and finally closing the door even to his most intimate friends. He rarely went out, and then only at night, when he went to visit the old bookshops in quest of the volumes of ghostly lore and demonology which, towards the end, were his only reading.

Nelson Browne also admits that Le Fanu had almost completely withdrawn from contact with his fellows in the last years of his life, finding 'the present so painful and the future so ominous that he could live emotionally only in the past'. On the other hand, he records that Le Fanu was in his prime 'an accurate man of business', given even in his later years to 'the old, puckish love of leg-pulling and practical joking', and quite 'the beau ideal of an Irish wit and scholar of the old school'; and he certainly married and had four children, which at least argues a conventionally stable domestic life. Moreover, even if Le Fanu did exhibit convincingly neurotic symptoms towards the end of his life, his artistic powers were nonetheless at their peak of cool and stylish perfection, and in any event most of his occult stories had been written far earlier, when his way of life showed every external sign of maturity, cultivation and general contentment with his lot. At the same time, it is unquestionably true that Le Fanu did have an abiding concern with the occult, which is not necessarily a sign of incipient neurosis, and also with the physically horrible, which certainly is hardly a sign of psychological stability.

One of the major merits of his short stories of the occult is indeed the fact that they embody symbols of psychological repression which positively anticipate the work of Freud. For example, in *Green Tea*, the story which V. S. Pritchett praises so highly, an apparently harmless and well-intentioned old clergyman is driven to his death by the apparition of a monkey which keeps materializing before him whenever his constitution is weakened by excessive consumption of green tea. He has no idea how to deal with the apparition, because he has no idea what it represents. Nor does Le Fanu himself attempt to define precisely the symbolism of the monkey. The post-Freudian reader however easily recognizes the hideous, hairy little animal as an image of the old cleric's repressed sexual desires, which have been banished to his unconscious for so long that he has literally forgotten that he ever had them.

The idea that nature, denied normal expression, will reassert itself in an abnormal and indeed unrecognizable form, is given even more subtle, and thus more effective expression in *The Familiar*. Captain Barton has once caused the death of a sailor by having him flogged with excessive violence, apparently to stop the man from bothering Barton about the fate of his daughter, who had

loved the captain and been abandoned by him. Barton
returns home, becomes engaged to another girl, and is
thereupon haunted by a phantasm of the dead sailor, whose
physical appearance is far smaller than the actual body
of the man when he was alive. The figure is obviously a
hallucination of Barton's tremendous and repressed feelings of guilt over his treatment of both the sailor and his
daughter. The altered size of the figure may simply be
intended to serve as a reminder that it is in fact something
outside the limits of normal nature. Also, to the extent
that it represents Barton's conscience, it might symbolize
the fact that in the past at least his conscience was far
less powerful than his desires. One remembers that the
evil Mr Hyde in Stevenson's story was physically smaller
than the ostensibly good Dr Jekyll, because Jekyll had in
the past exercised his good propensities to a greater extent
than his evil ones.

The other short stories of the occult generally lack this
element of symbolism. Tales such as *Madame Crowl's
Ghost, Mr Justice Harbottle* and *Some Strange Disturb-
ances in an Old House in Aungier Street* are in essence
simply superbly told tales, written with restraint, a flaw-
less ear for dialect and humour, and a well-nigh perfect
prose style which is graceful, lucid, idiomatic, musical and
above all controlled. It is indeed this extreme sensitivity
and fastidiousness of expression that makes Le Fanu's
obsession with crude physical horror all the more incongruous and disturbing. Probably no writer of any literary
pretensions has exhibited a more clinical concern with the
physically repellent, and the subtlety with which he treats
this aspect on occasion makes it only the more ugly. For
example, the horror of the episode in *Uncle Silas* where
Dudley Ruthyn stoves in Madame de la Rougierre's head
with a geological hammer is intensified by the fact that
the narrator does not actually witness the event, but
instead hears the attendant noises. In the same manner,

one hears rather than sees the trepanning operation in *The House by the Churchyard.*

But Le Fanu can also be extremely explicit in visual details. The episode in *Checkmate* where the wicked baron shows David Arden the plaster masks, mementoes of the gruesome plastic surgery which transformed the handsome murderer Yelland Mace into the hideously fascinating Mr Longcluse, is as ugly as precision can make it. But Le Fanu can be more clinical still. Colonel Gaillarde, in *The Room at the Dragon Volant*, is described as having 'the palest face I ever saw. It was broad, ugly and malignant. . . . Across the nose and eyebrow there was a deep scar, which made the repulsive face grimmer.' The Colonel apparently acquired his complexion at Ligny, where 'a bit of a shell cut me across the leg and opened an artery. It was spouting as high as a chimney and in half a minute I had lost enough to fill a pitcher. . . . I lost so much blood, I have been as pale as the bottom of a plate ever since.' The Colonel however is surpassed for sheer physical unattractiveness by 'Mr Burton in deshabille' in *The Strange Adventure of Miss Laura Mildmay*:

> Mr Burton's teeth were gone, and his left eye was out, and a deep ugly hole was in the place of that organ. He had screwed his mouth into a deep grimace, and his face looked ever so broad, and ever so short.
>
> His whole face was crimson with the fire of brandy. . . . His lips were pursed and working, as they will over toothless gums. The blank eye puzzled the baronet, and the other pierced him with a gleam of fire.
>
> On the dressing-table close by were two tumblers of water, in one of which were Mr Burton's teeth, and in the other his glass eye.

One could hardly deny that Le Fanu had a taste for the morbid.

This might not in itself have led him to the vampire legend, although a taste for vampires might indeed seem to imply a certain constitutional morbidity. The decisive element here is Le Fanu's other predominating characteristic. It is perhaps not precisely accurate to say that Le Fanu was obsessed by lesbianism. The position is rather that he seems to have been virtually incapable of conceiving any kind of erotic or even emotional relationship in anything other than lesbian terms. He is admittedly not the only Victorian novelist to be preoccupied with the physical expression of emotional relationships between women. Intense and in effect passionate relationships of this kind occur in almost all the major novels of Dickens and Meredith, and on a considerably more subdued emotional level even in Trollope.[2] Le Fanu, however, carries this approach to the point of making his heroes sound like transvestites; in fact he has no heroes in the conventional sense. There are instead strange, ostensibly male figures, insistently androgynous, and also characteristically instruments of destruction. For example Guy Deverell, in the book of that name, is described as being 'tall, slender, rather dark, and decidedly handsome', with a voice 'sweet but peculiar', and 'a clear, melancholy face, with ... large eyes and wavy hair'. Deverell is also a symbol of ferocious and unrelenting vengeance, wielded by the monstrous Varbarriere. Stanley Lake in *Wylder's Hand*, which is quite literally a story of lesbian love, is 'rather handsome', with 'eyes very peculiar both in shape and colour, and something of elegance of finish in his other features, and of general grace in the *coup d'oeil*'. He also has 'a singularly pale face', is physically small and delicate, is lacking 'in a few manly points of character', and is a crook and a murderer. Walter Longcluse is thin, tall, pale, with thin, pale lips, and is also a murderer. Alfred Dacre, in *Haunted Lives*, is frail, exotic, Italianate in appearance, a delicate musician, a graceful conversa-

B

tionalist, and is described throughout in such feminine terms, as regards both his physical appearance and his personal qualities, that one can only imagine that Le Fanu had conceived the character as a woman in disguise, suddenly realized the complications that this was going to involve when he has Dacre apparently fall in love with the heroine, and resolved the problem by having Dacre die unknown in a debtor's prison. There is no hero at all in Le Fanu's most popular novel, *Uncle Silas*, and the only approach the heroine has to any kind of relationship with men is when she is about to be molested as a child by local gypsies.

It is thus rather surprising that Peter Penzoldt should suggest not only that it is doubtful whether Le Fanu ever knew of the technical term 'lesbianism', but that he might not even have been 'aware of the true nature of what he was describing'. It is far more likely that he was so well aware of what he was describing that he deliberately seized on the vampire myth as quite literally the only way in which he could effectively develop this particular theme. It is a very short and very logical step from Guy Deverell and Alfred Dacre to the evocation of Elizabeth Bathory.

If this was Le Fanu's problem, then he solved it with technical perfection in *Carmilla*. There was really no need for anybody ever to write another vampire story. Everything composed since has been only a variation on the themes developed in that novelette. Everything composed since has in fact been only plagiarism, conscious or otherwise. All the ingredients are present in classic form. There is the young, beautiful and incredibly unintelligent heroine; the quaint old Gothic family *schloss* somewhere in Eastern Europe; the equally beautiful female predatory demon, the descendant of a vanished aristocratic family; the dear old general, whose own daughter had been an earlier victim of the demon; and the wise old doctor, skilled in the lore of the vampire and the strategy of coping with this particular menace, or epidemic as it is technically termed. All the physical and hydraulic absurdities are also present: the vampire has a grasp which paralyses human limbs; it has the power to rise spotless and fragrant, without bathing or changing its clothes, after lying all day in seven inches of blood, which interestingly never coagulates; and it can be put down only by having a stake driven through its heart and then being decapitated. There is also of course the phoney historical background, expounded with a sense of style and conviction which Le Fanu's imitators could never approach.

Above all there is also the element of erotic symbolism. This is explicit to a degree which can only be termed fantastic, in the context of the times. We have for example this description of the approaches of the vampire Carmilla to the unnamed heroine:

> She used to place her pretty arms about my neck, draw me to her, and laying her cheek to mine, murmur with her lips near my ear, 'Dearest, your little heart is wounded; think me not cruel because I obey the irresistible law of my strength and weakness; if your dear heart is wounded, my wild heart bleeds with yours. In the rapture of my enormous humiliation I live in your warm life, and you shall die – die, sweetly die – into mine.' And when she had spoken such a rhapsody, she would press me more closely in her trembling embrace, and her lips in soft kisses gently glow upon my cheek.... Sometimes after an hour of apathy, my strange and beautiful companion would take my hand and hold it with a fond pressure, renewed again and again; blushing softly, gazing in my face with languid and burning eyes, and breathing so fast that her dress rose and fell with the tumultuous respiration. It was like the ardour of a lover; it embarrassed

me; it was hateful and yet over-powering; and with gloating eyes she drew me to her, and her hot lips travelled along my cheek in kisses; and she would whisper, almost in sobs, 'You are mine, you *shall* be mine.'

This is far more specific than any scene of heterosexual passion depicted in the pages of nineteenth-century fiction, other than in overt pornography. The sense of physical excitement is conveyed by the structure of the sentences as well as by the words, which can hardly happen without conscious intention on the part of the writer. In any case, Le Fanu repeatedly makes the vampire speak unambiguously about her love for the heroine: she loves only her; she wishes to spend her whole life loving her; and she wishes to continue to possess the heroine after death, whether she receives only hatred in return or not. Carmilla also speaks of her 'humiliation', which may imply the physical nature of the act through which her love has to be expressed, but more likely simply refers to the totality of her obsession with the heroine. These, one might note, are sentiments most uncharacteristic of a vampire: the nature of the species from all other accounts is to be motivated only by thirst, and its sole concern for the welfare of the victim is that the victim should not die too soon, thereby depriving the vampire of the means of slaking its thirst. A vampire does not experience emotions. Carmilla on the other hand is both predatory and emotionally involved. The truth of the matter is that Carmilla is obviously conceived not as a demon, but as a woman, totally absorbed, physically and emotionally, by her passion for another woman. Nor is the heroine herself wholly unresponsive to Carmilla's advances: she is fascinated by her beauty, and enjoys stroking and playing with her hair. Their moment of physical union is described in the most remarkable passage in Victorian fiction:

Certain vague and strange sensations visited me in my sleep. The prevailing one was of that pleasant, peculiar cold thrill which we feel in bathing, when we move against the current of a river. This was soon accompanied by dreams that seemed interminable. . . . Sometimes there came a sensation as if a hand was drawn softly along my cheek and neck. Sometimes it was as if warm lips kissed me, and longer and more lovingly as they reached my throat, but there the caress fixed itself. My heart beat faster, my breathing rose and fell rapidly and full drawn; a sobbing, that rose into a sense of strangulation, supervened, and turned into a dreadful convulsion, in which my senses left me and I became unconscious.

There is no possible doubt as to what Le Fanu is describing: the passage depicts an act of oral sex, carried to the point of orgasm. The writing is not only composed with obvious feeling; it is also deeply pondered, and crammed with extraordinarily precise detail. One can only wonder where Le Fanu got his data from. He certainly did not get them from anybody who had been dined on by a vampire.

The vampire legend thus takes flight through the medium of Le Fanu's art, as a symbol of predatory lesbianism and oral sex. There is also a slight but explicit undercurrent of social commentary, in that the vampire-lady is an aristocrat, who preys on her social inferiors after death, as she and her ancestors preyed on them while they were among the living. This sub-theme is indeed not fully developed: we are not informed of the symbolic role of those peasants who have been drained to death by the aristocratic vampires, and have in consequence become vampires in their own right. Perhaps they act as the lackeys of the aristocratic demons after death. It is not really important. What is important is that Le Fanu should have devised a totally effective erotic symbol with consummate literary art, permitting the presentation of themes which could not possibly even be alluded to under the social and aesthetic conventions of the time. The treatment of physical passion between women could be permissible in Victorian times only if it were made clear that one of the women was dead. Now that the theme can be discussed, we presumably have no further need of the symbol. Permissiveness has made the vampire story obsolete, even if Le Fanu's art had not already made it superfluous.

One should not however rate Le Fanu's achievement too highly. He has undoubtedly a great deal to offer, much of it unavailable in other writers of his time. He has an almost perfect, muted, musical prose style, immensely evocative without recourse to rhetoric. His treatment of dialect is impeccable and his eroticism is the most seductive in Victorian fiction. He has written some of the best stories of occult and also of high adventure in English. At the same time, his own baffling temperament can only limit his appeal. One rapidly becomes dissatisfied with a novelist who seems to be concerned with eroticism in any sense only in terms of lesbians, transvestites and child molesters. It is not entirely unfair to Le Fanu that he should be remembered largely as the man whose stories have inspired almost as many worthless and sadistic books and films as *Dracula* itself. It was the kind of company he kept.

3 Sex and Horror: Bram Stoker

Bram Stoker's *Dracula* is by any financial standard incomparably the most successful story of the occult ever written. Critics, historians and aficionados can always find something of interest in Le Fanu, but the enduring fame of Stoker's novel rests on the soundest possible base: its unflagging popularity with the general reading public. *Dracula* has in fact never been out of print since its first appearance in 1897; it has undoubtedly inspired more films than any other work of fiction, and it shares with Le Fanu's *Carmilla* the distinction of being the most frequently and shamelessly plagiarized work of English fiction. It would be impossible to try to list the varieties of the Dracula story which have been presented since Stoker's death, either in fiction or on the screen. One might simply say that the Vampire King has been depicted in almost every conceivable aspect. We have had the opportunity in fiction to enjoy, if that is the word, the adventures of *Dracula's Gold*, *Dracula's Scars*, *Dracula's Bride*, *Dracula's Daughters*, *Dracula's Drums*, *Dracula's Brothers*, and *Blacula*, a negro vampire. However, there is an important difference between Stoker and Le Fanu in that the numerous recent plagiarists of the latter are far more likely to have been inspired by the film version of *Carmilla* (*The Vampire Lovers*) than by the book itself, while most of those writers who have felt that there was money to be made by inventing new chronicles of the Vampire King would seem to have worked to some extent from the original text. Stoker has always been read, while Le Fanu has very frequently not.

No book could possibly have been so successful without possessing some extraordinary features. Some of the most singular of these in fact concern the author. Stoker, the most successful of the occult novelists, was also in many ways the most atypical. His life and in many ways his personality would have been fully appropriate for a hero of John Buchan, Conan Doyle or Anthony Hope. He was virtually the ideal conventional late-Victorian and Edwardian type: well-educated, scholastically brilliant, athletic, articulate, a man of affairs, believing in if not always practising the most admirable domestic virtues, and also witty and charming, according to the testimony of his friends, although no two qualities could be less apparent in his writings. He was born in 1847; educated at Dublin University, where he became president of the historical and philosophical societies, receiving academic honours in oratory, composition and, improbably, pure mathematics; was a crack athlete who retained enormous physical strength until the last; and moved in his professional life from law to the stage and finally to journalism. In 1878 he became the acting manager of Sir Henry Irving, in which capacity he must have been the most industrious secretary in the history of the human race, claiming to have been responsible for despatching about half a million letters. Nobody who lived this kind of life could well have found much time even to think about the writing of imaginative fiction. In fact, the only writing which Stoker did outside the course of duty before the age of fifty was a public service handbook entitled *The Duties of Clerks of Petty Sessions* and a collection of singularly grim and ponderous fairy stories called *Under the Sunset. Dracula* was thus in no way the creation of a sickly and youthful recluse, as one might well have imagined; it was the work of a robustly powerful, sociable and enormously busy man in the prime of life.

In fact Stoker was in every way suited to be quite a different kind of writer: he had the physical resources as well as the disposition for a life of high adventure, and one might note that his heroes, who are customarily globe-trotters of quite abnormal physical equipment, become credible only when smiting the ungodly with bowie knife, slavonic sword or Ghurkha *kukri*. Had he been born thirty years later, Stoker might well have found his true forte as a competitor of Biggles, in fiction and even possibly in real life. His commitment to occult fiction seems to have been brought about entirely by a couple of sufficiently intriguing accidents. By mere chance, Stoker met Professor Armin Vambery of Budapest in London in 1891, and became fascinated by his stories of the eastern marches of the Austro-Hungarian Empire. These stories naturally included the vampire legend, to which Countess Elizabeth Bathory had given such *éclat*. Not surprisingly, Vambery's stories inspired a nightmare, in which Stoker was confronted by the vision of a Vampire King rising from his grave. *Dracula* was in flight.

The dazzling initial success of the story was no doubt helped by the accident of timing. One could hardly suggest that the world ever actually needed another vampire story, but the 1890s were a period remarkably receptive to what *Dracula* had to offer: there was a booming market in the occult, in tales of adventure or detection, and in stories of exploration or historical romance. *Dracula* scored in all these departments. On the occult side, it presented a full-length novel, longer and far more flamboyant than anything Le Fanu had attempted. On the exotic side, it was set largely in legendary Transylvania, an area only recently investigated by wandering Englishmen and for practical purposes fully as remote and far more unfamiliar than the heart of Africa. As a historical romance, it contains passages of narrative of ancient battles and lost causes nonetheless compelling for being wildly inaccurate in almost every possible way.

We Szekelys, [Dracula tells the hero], have a right to be proud, for in our veins flows the blood of many brave races who fought as the lion fights, for lordship. Here, in the whirlpool of European races, the Ugric tribe bore down from Iceland the fighting spirit which Thor and Wodin gave them, which their Berserkers displayed to such fell intent on the seaboards of Europe. ... Here, too, when they came, they found the Huns, whose warlike fury had swept the earth like a living flame.... It is no wonder that we were a conquering race; that we were proud; that when the Magyar, the Lombard, the Avar, the Bulgar, or the Turk poured his thousands on our frontiers, we drove them back?... When was redeemed that great shame of my nation, the shame of Cassova, when the flags of the Wallach and the Magyar went down beneath the Crescent, who was it but one of my own race who as Voivode crossed the Danube and beat the Turk on his own ground? This was a Dracula indeed!

Unfortunately, he was not a Dracula at all, strictly speaking. Most characteristically, Stoker failed to do his homework properly. The ancestor whom the Vampire is lauding was probably Vlad III of Wallachia, who flourished between the years of 1436 and 1446, and was known as Dracul, signifying a descendant of Genghis Khan. The first Dracula in fact was his successor, Vlad v, who reigned during the periods 1456–62 and 1475–6, and signed his correspondence Vlad Dracula, using the feminine '–a' ending, which incongruously could signify descent from a person of rank when used by a man. It was this Vlad Dracula who has been the chief inspiration of Rumanian

horror stories for some five hundred years, not indeed
primarily because of any association with the cult of the
vampire, but because of his favoured outdoor activity
during his life, as a result of which he became known as
Vlad Tepes, or Vlad the Impaler. He appears to have
made sport of literally hundreds and even thousands of his
subjects in this manner, being particularly fond of dining
outdoors, surrounded by a veritable forest of impaled
men, women and children. According to one account,
Vlad remarked, 'Oh, what great gracefulness they
exhibit!' as he watched his victims writhe in their death
agonies. On any account, Vlad v's genuinely demoniac
qualities seem to have excelled the efforts of all alleged
vampires put together. He is incidentally admired as a
Rumanian hero of the first order by the present regime
in Bucharest, who regard him as proving the theory that
Rumania can prosper only under authoritarian rule.

One would have thought that Stoker would have made
some reference to Vlad's impalement fixation if he had
known about it. The story of Dracula developed under
Stoker's hands as a work of erotic imagery above all else,
and there can hardly be a more powerful erotic image
than impalement. One can only assume that Stoker knew
even less about Eastern Europe and its history than might
have been imagined.

It did not matter at all. What was important was that
the past history of the Dracula family should sound
authentic enough to give verisimilitude to a story of otherwise incredible adventure, and Stoker succeeded in doing
so adequately for the purpose in hand. There was little
danger that anybody was going to check his facts at the
time, anyway. But fascinatingly inaccurate historical and
geographical data could make only marginal contributions to the triumph of the new legend of the vampire
king. Far more important was Stoker's use of an amaz-
ingly complex narrative technique, never even hinted at

in his previous writings and never employed so successfully in his later work. This was the technique, used by Samuel Richardson and Tobias Smollett at enormous length in the eighteenth century and refined considerably by Wilkie Collins in the nineteenth, of weaving together what purport to be accounts written by personages in the story themselves, in the form of diaries, personal letters, legal testimonies and the like. On the face of it, such an approach is about as realistic as grand opera; it means, as J. B. Priestley points out, that characters are supposed to be writing letters or making up their daily journals when they should be screaming for help or running for the police. It does however have enormous narrative advantages: it provides the immediacy of the first person without the necessary limitations imposed by the use of a single narrator, and it is the easiest of all ways to reveal character, quite apart from its own inherent technical interest for the reader. *Dracula* is in fact probably the most remarkable example of the multi-narrative novel in English; the story is conveyed through the media of four journals, three exchanges of correspondence, two newspaper reports, a phonograph record and a ship's log.

This remarkable display of literary technique is all the more impressive because Stoker really exhibits no other literary skills whatever. He has in the first place the deficiency commonly found among writers who concern themselves almost exclusively with occult themes, of having either no interest in human personality, or no ability to analyze it. Despite the fact that he uses with unsurpassed skill the technique most suited to revelation of character, the people in the story are totally unconvincing, with the partial exception of the demon himself, whose personality is of course inhuman. Jonathon Harker, the hero, is supposed to be a powerful man of action, ever ready to smite the powers of evil with his *kukri*. His journal reveals him as timid, half-witted and literally without any distinguishing traits at all. Two other subordinate heroes, Lord Godalming and 'our old pal at the Korea, Jack Seward', exist only as names. Their ally, Quincy P. Morris, is indeed memorable, because he says things like: 'Miss Lucy, I know I ain't good enough to regulate the fixin's of your little shoes, but I guess if you wait till you find a man that is you will go join them seven young women with the lamps when you quit. Won't you just hitch up alongside of me and let us go down the road together, driving in double harness?' Stoker may well be the worst writer of regional dialogue in English. This is the more unfortunate in that the only person in the story whom Stoker attempts to endow with archetypal qualities apart from Dracula himself is the vampire hunter Van Hesling, 'the great specialist . . . a philosopher and a metaphysician, and one of the most advanced scientists of his day', who expresses himself in a kind of delicatessen Dutch: 'Now take down our brave young lover, give him of the port wine, and let him lie down a while. . . . Oh, little miss, my dear, do not fear me. I only do for your good; but there is much virtue to you in those so common flower.' As for the women, it must be said that Lucy Westenra and Mina Harker acquire the faintest interest as human beings only when they begin to turn into vampires.

Even the basic story itself exhibits amazing depths of incompetence, apart from the inexplicable technical brilliance of the multi-narrative structure. For example, Stoker's description of the archetype Van Hesling, which is perhaps the best thing in the book, does not occur until long after the philosopher's first appearance. Even worse, the opening account of Jonathon Harker's first encounter with the vampire is an unconscious masterpiece of un-intended humour, and it is disturbing to imagine that Stoker really cannot have seen the comic aspect of a hero who insists on completing his journal to Castle

Dracula after an experience such as the following:

> When I asked him if he knew Count Dracula, and could tell me anything of his castle, both he and his wife crossed themselves and ... refused to speak further. ... Just before I was leaving, the old lady came up to my room and said in a very hysterical way: 'Must you go? Oh! young Herr, must you go? ... tonight, when the clock strikes midnight, all the evil things in the world will have full sway! Do you know where you are going and what you are going to?

As he obviously does not, she gives him a crucifix, while the locals come and look at Harker, 'most of them pityingly', as indeed they might.

> I could hear a lot of words often repeated ... so I quietly got my polyglot dictionary from my bag and looked them out. I must say they were not cheering to me, for amongst them were 'Ordog' – Satan, 'pokol' – hell, 'stregoica' – witch, 'vrolok' and 'vlkoslak' – both mean the same thing, one being Slovak and the other Servian for something that is either werewolf or vampire. (*Mem.* I must ask the Count about these superstitions.)

Even Harker might have guessed by this time that while the Count would no doubt be able to speak with some authority about those particular superstitions, he might not necessarily have been the best person to ask. But worse is to come. As Harker prepares to leave, the villagers all gather around him, 'making the sign of the cross and pointing two fingers towards him. When he understandably asks what the latter gesture meant he is told that it is a charm or guard against the evil eye. One can only feel that anybody who continued on such a journey to such a destination at such a time after receiving such discouragement, really deserved to have Dracula and his family waiting for him at the end.

It is really impossible to burlesque the opening narrative

of *Dracula*. Stoker has done it already. But the most amazing lapse in the whole book is the failure to provide any explanation of how Harker actually escapes from Castle Dracula. Stoker's descriptions are of course totally imprecise, but we are at least told that 'a stone falling from the window would fall a thousand feet without touching anything', and that when Dracula himself leaves his apartment, by the window, naturally, and head first, he went 'a hundred feet straight down before vanishing into some hole or window'. This would be no problem for the Count, who of course could fly. It would have been something else for Harker who could not fly, whose rooms must have been higher up, and who would have had to complete the journey to the ground. The technical difficulties were obviously too much for Stoker, who offers no suggestion at all as to how the feat was accomplished. Perhaps Harker also went head first; on his own testimony, he need have had no fear of brain damage.

Apart from all these glaring absurdities, there are certain inherent difficulties in treating seriously with the vampire legend itself. Stoker certainly tries to give maximum credibility to the myth by larding it with alleged historical and clinical detail, much of which admittedly loses its force through being presented in the fractured English of Van Hesling:

Take it, then, that the vampire, and the belief in his limitations and his cure, rest for the moment on the same base. For, let me tell you, he is known everywhere that men have been. In old Greece, in old Rome; he flourish in Germany all over, in France, in India, even in the Chersonese; and in China, so far from us in all ways, there even is he, and the peoples fear him at this day. He have follow the wake of the berserker Icelander, the devil-begotten Hun, the Slav, the Saxon, the Magyar.

This is well enough; but Stoker then proceeds to destroy the effect with an account of the natural history of the vampire. The species has indeed many excellent survival qualities: it does not die from the effects of time; it does not eat; it does not throw a shadow or reflection; it can metamorphose itself into a bat, a dog or a cloud of luminous dust, among other things; it can see in the dark; and it has the strength of ten normal men. However, it also suffers from serious limitations: as Van Hesling puts it, the vampire

> may not enter anywhere at the first, unless there be some one of the household who bid him to come . . . His power ceases, as does that of all evil things, at the coming of the day. . . . If he be not at the place whither he is bound, he can only change himself at noon or at exact sunrise or sunset . . . he can only pass running water at the slack or the flood of the tide. Then there are things which so afflict him that he has no power, as the garlic that we know of, and as for things sacred, as this symbol, my crucifix, that was amongst us even now when we resolve, to them he is nothing. . . . The branch of a wild rose on his coffin keep him that he move not from it; a sacred bullet fired into the coffin kill him so that he be true dead; and as for the stake through him, we already know of its peace; or the cut-off head that giveth rest.

We also know, even if Van Hesling did not, about the boiled head in vinegar which brings peace to the Cretan *kathanko*, the poppyseed in the grave which kills the Prussian *gunach* and the lemon in the mouth which gives rest to the Saxon *neuntatu*. The pursuit of the vampire begins to sound increasingly agricultural. Nor is this element of absurdity aided by the fact that Stoker makes Dracula travel to England by ship, accompanied by fifty boxes of earth. The tale of the voyage itself is very effec-

tively horrifying, apart from the slight implausibility of a
ship's captain who really begins to panic only after seven
of his crew of nine have disappeared into thin air. However, the spell is broken immediately by the discovery that
Dracula's first activities in England are in fact in the
realms of real estate: he needs conveniently situated lots
in which to locate his fifty boxes of Transylvanian earth, in
which he needs to bury himself for some part of each day.
Stoker really has no sense of the ridiculous at all.

With all these deficiencies, *Dracula* obviously needed
more than mere technical skill to make it the best-selling
story of the occult ever written. Its success is due in the
end to two main elements. First and by far the less important is the uncomplicated appeal of a tale of sheer high
adventure, culminating in the clash of bowie knife and
kukri against Szgany steel at the Iron Gates. However,
this kind of thing is more frequently and more competently described in the novels of Arthur Conan Doyle,
Robert Louis Stevenson, Anthony Hope, Grant Allen and
half a dozen other writers of the time. What one does not
find in them is the towering erotic symbolism, which is
what *Dracula* is actually all about.

The eroticism is explicit, coherent and obsessional. The
story is quite simply about the legendary confrontation
between sacred and profane love, based on the assumption, common among those who have never read Plato or
never understood him, that the profane is necessarily the
erotic, and the sacred is something else. The vampires,
both male and female, are incarnations of sexual desire.
'Voluptuous' is Stoker's favourite and indeed almost his
only adjective for the physical appearance of the vampire,
and the quality of voluptuousness is consistently presented
as residing chiefly in the vampire's lips and mouth. The
oral fixation is total. The vampire ladies who appear
before Harker at Castle Dracula do indeed differ in other
physical characteristics, two being dark, with 'great, dark,

piercing eyes, that seemed almost red', while the third 'was fair, as fair can be, with great, wavy masses of golden hair'; but

> all three had brilliant white teeth, that shone like pearls against the ruby red of their voluptuous lips.... I felt in my heart a wicked, burning desire that they would kiss me with those red lips.... The fair girl advanced and bent over me till I could feel the movement of her breath upon me.... The girl went on her knees, and bent over me, fairly gloating. There was a deliberate voluptuousness which was both thrilling and repulsive, and as she arched her neck she actually licked her lips like an animal, till I could see in the moonlight the moisture shining on the scarlet lips and on the red tongue as it lapped the white sharp teeth. Lower and lower went her head.... Then she paused, and I could hear the churning sound of her tongue as it lapped the white sharp teeth and lips. . . . I closed my eyes in a languorous ecstasy and waited – waited with beating heart.

Even allowing for the fact that Stoker is a worse writer than one would have believed possible, the obsessive repetition of certain words and actions, associated with the emotions attributed to Harker and the vampire, make the passage the literary equivalent of an orgasm. Still more significant however is the extraordinary precision of detail, which could only have come from actual observation: while 'churning' may not be the ideal word to describe the sound that a tongue makes when moving over teeth, it could hardly have occurred to Stoker in the first place if he had not listened intently to the sound itself. One can only assume in fact that Stoker is writing the whole scene from personal experience. As he could never have been dined on by a vampire himself, he could in practice only be recalling an experience of oral sex, to

which he may have been treated by the prostitutes he is
known to have had dealings with in Paris and London.
As in the passage from *Carmilla* such a scene could have
been included in a book sold over the counter in Victorian
England only because it purported to describe what it felt
like to be assaulted by a vampire.

Stoker also finds material in the vampire legend for
symbols of genital sex. The impalement of Lucy Westenra
in her capacity as vampire, is presented as an episode of
sadistic rape, culminating in mutual orgasm. In a scene
for which the appropriate background music could only
be the Anvil Chorus,

> Arthur took the stake and the hammer ... [he] placed
> the point over the heart, and as I looked I could see its
> dint in the white flesh. Then he struck with all his
> might. The Thing in the coffin writhed; and a hideous,
> blood-curdling screech came from the opened red lips.
> The body shook and twisted in wild contortions; the
> sharp white teeth champed together till the lips were
> cut, and the mouth was smeared with a crimson foam.
> But Arthur never faltered. He looked like a figure of
> Thor as his untrembling arm rose and fell, driving
> deeper and deeper the mercy-bearing stake.... His face
> was set, and high duty seemed to shine through it. . . .
> And then the writhing and quivering of the body
> became less, and the teeth seemed to champ and the
> face to quiver.... He reeled and would have fallen had
> we not caught him. The great drops of sweat sprang
> from his forehead, and his breath came in broken gasps.

Lucy also is at peace, having experienced her first and
presumably her last climax: 'a holy calm . . . lay like sun-
shine over the wasted face and form'.

It has already been said that Stoker's women become
attractive only when they become vampires. Lucy
Westenra, about to die into vampirehood, says to her love

'in a soft voluptuous voice, such as I had never heard from her lips: "Arthur! Oh, my love, I am so glad you have come! Kiss me!"' As a fully-fledged vampire, she is still more voluptuous, being known to her child victims as the 'bloofer lady', a phrase borrowed not quite accurately from Dickens. When she is found prowling in the churchyard, 'her eyes blazed with unholy light, and the face became wreathed with a voluptuous smile'; she speaks with 'a languorous, voluptuous grace', through a 'bloodstained, voluptuous mouth', which seems 'a devilish mockery of Lucy's sweet purity'. Nothing could make Mina Harker voluptuous, but Van Hesling notes that she 'still sleep, and sleep; and she look in her sleep more healthy and more redder than before. And I like it not.' Dracula himself has lips 'whose remarkable ruddiness showed extraordinary vitality in a man of his years'. But the most revealing description of the Vampire King is that given by Mina Harker, seeing him for the first time after he has landed in London:

> I was looking at a very beautiful girl, in a big cart-wheel hat, sitting in a victoria outside Giuliano's, when I felt Jonathon clutch my arm ... he gazed at a tall, thin man, with a beaky nose and black moustache and pointed beard, who was also observing the pretty girl. He was looking at her so hard that he did not see either of us, and so I had a good view of him. His face was not a good face: it was hard, and cruel, and sensual, and his big white teeth, that looked all the whiter because his lips were so red, were pointed like an animal's.... He kept staring; a man came out of the shop with a small parcel, and gave it to the lady, who then drove off. The dark man kept his eyes fixed on her, and when the carriage moved up Piccadilly he followed in the same direction, and hailed a hansom.

The image of the vampire as masher could not be more

complete: nobody reading this passage in isolation could possibly imagine that the sole motivation inspiring the tall, thin man with the red lips who was so assiduously pursuing the beautiful girl in the big hat was in fact a terrible thirst.

Dracula was in many ways a triumph of eroticism over incompetence. It is not surprising that Stoker was never able to repeat it. His other occult novels are singular examples of his capacity to nullify potentially exciting plots by sheer bad writing. The most popular next to *Dracula* was *The Jewel of Seven Stars*, which had indeed an ideal motif for a story of high adventure. The hero, a young barrister, is summoned at midnight from his rooms in Jermyn Street; he hastens to Kensington Palace Road where a mysterious and apparently murderous assault has been made upon a famous Egyptologist, whose beautiful daughter is conveniently in love with him. The police are called in and the Egyptologist is found to be on the brink of completing an experiment to bring back to life the mummy of Queen Tera, a fabulous Egyptian beauty, somewhat over-endowed in the sense of possessing seven fingers on each hand, and seven toes on each foot. Unfortunately, literally nothing happens: there is almost no dialogue, no attempt at characterization, virtually no action and nothing but anti-climax at the end.

Nor oddly is there anything in the nature of erotic symbolism. The sweltering sexuality of *Dracula* is totally absent from *The Jewel of Seven Stars*. It does return, albeit very allusively, in *The Lady of The Shroud*, which in many ways is the best story that Stoker ever wrote, but which can hardly be considered as a novel of the occult, despite the ghoulishness of the title, since the whole point of the action turns on the hero's discovery that his lover is not the vampire he thought she was.

However sex and the occult provide the mainsprings of the plot of Stoker's last and by far his worst novel, *The*

Lair of the White Worm, published posthumously in 1912. Howard P. Lovecraft comments that this book 'utterly ruins a magnificent idea by a development almost infantile'.[1] One may or may not agree with this valuation of the idea, but there is no doubt about Stoker's ability to ruin it. He does indeed lose control of the story to such an extent that it is really impossible to know what he actually thought he was writing about. The initial concept involves the hunt for a gigantic snake, surviving underground from what Stoker vaguely calls 'the geologic age – the great birth and growth of the world, when natural forces ran riot, and when the struggle for existence was so savage that no vitality which was not founded in a gigantic form could have even a possibility of survival'. The existence of such a creature is apparently alluded to in some of the legends of Mercia. The dramatic possibilities of the situation should have been heightened by the suggestion that the snake or 'White Worm' has acquired occult powers over one of the local heiresses: 'if my theory is correct,' the hero's grand-uncle explains, ' the once beautiful human body of Lady Arabella is under the control of this ghastly White Worm.' Stoker presumably means 'once human' rather than 'once beautiful', since Lady Arabella is undoubtedly attractive, although in an emphatically serpentine manner: she first appears 'clad in some form of soft white stuff which clung to her form, showing to the full every movement of her sinuous figure'. She also has long, flexible white hands, which she employs 'with a strange movement as of waving to and fro'. Still more significantly, she is attacked on sight by the mongooses accompanying the hunters of the White Worm. She conventionally shoots the first one. However, she seizes the second in her hands, 'and with a fury superior to its own, tore it in two just as it had been a sheet of paper. The strength used for such an act must have been terrific.'

Lady Arabella and the White Worm are only part of the story, however. There is also an objectionable land-owner, Caswell, who is hated by the local farmers for apparently quite inconsistent reasons. They hate him in the first place because he has an occult quality of attract-ing birds, but they hate him even more after he saves their crops by driving the birds away with a huge kite, shaped like a great hawk. He also has a monstrous ser-vant Oolanga, whose face 'was unreformed, unsoftened savage, and inherent in it were all the hideous possibilities of a lost, devil-ridden child of the forest and the swamp – the lowest of all created things that could be regarded as in some form ostensibly human.' Unfortunately after this promising introduction, Oolanga never actually does any-thing. Neither does Caswell, despite his having evil inten-tions towards two local girls, Lilla and Mima Watford, who are so far from being developed as characters that they are not even given any dialogue. Lilla Watford is however considered sufficiently important by Lady Arabella to require killing off, after which the snake-lady 'tore off her clothes with feverish fingers, and in full enjoyment of her natural freedom, stretched her slim figure in animal delight'. At the end of the story, Cas-well's kite attracts a bolt of lightning which destroys the manor and its owner, and also presumably Lady Arabella, who has been lurking underneath in her capacity as the White Worm. It is really impossible to know what Stoker was trying to do in the story. All one can be sure of is that it could not possibly have been less competently written.

There is a brutally simple explanation for both the compelling eroticism of *Dracula* and the absolute nullity of his last story: as his great-nephew Daniel Farson dis-covered, Stoker actually died from the tertiary stage of syphilis before the *White Worm* was published, which would indicate that he contracted the disease some fifteen years before, or in 1897, the year in which *Dracula* was first published. Farson suggests further that Stoker had been driven into the company of 'other women, probably prostitutes among them', by the frigidity of his beautiful wife Florence, who appears to have refused to have sexual relations with Stoker after the first year of their marriage, during which their only child, Noel, was born. Florence undoubtedly seems to have been incredibly beautiful, incredibly vain and incredibly uninteresting. If she was also frigid, she could well have provided the model for Stoker's extremely boring heroines. By the same token, by driving Stoker into the arms of more accommodating and doubtless more adventurous ladies, she could also have indirectly provided him with models for his vastly more interesting vampires. The occult novel owes a substantial debt to Florence Stoker.

Farson's interpretation is certainly in accordance with all the known facts, chronologically and also psychologically. Stoker certainly contracted syphilis about the time that he wrote *Dracula*; he certainly had every reason to consort with prostitutes for at least a decade before that; and the tremendous eroticism of the book does indeed imply psychological stresses upon the author which would be consistent with the image of a highly conventional man driven by frustration and humiliation into unconventional ways. The vampires are presented as appallingly destructive demons incarnate; however they are also breathtakingly voluptuous and desirable; and their victims await their ministrations with ecstatic longing. The resulting commerce is disastrous for both parties: the victim dies and is corrupted into becoming a demon as well; and the demons are eventually exorcized by being decapitated if men, and impaled if women. The symbolism of guilt and frustration is well-nigh perfect.

The fact is that Stoker's achievement is a phenomenon of psychopathology rather than of literature. As a novelist,

Stoker had almost no sense of characterization, no sense
of prose style and no philosophical sense of the occult at
all.[2] What he did possess was a lively if hardly creative
imagination and, on one memorable occasion at least, a
remarkable mastery of the multi-narrative technique of
storytelling. He was able to put these qualities to the service
of the vampire legend to which he was introduced quite
fortuitously, at a time when he was emotionally harrowed
by sensations of guilt and frustration, very possibly heightened by the symptoms of the primary stages of syphilis
with their attendant feelings of anxiety and even horror.
He was thus uniquely fitted by time and circumstances to
give wings to the most effective image of erotic perversity
that the western consciousness has ever frightened itself
with. One should not of course exaggerate either the
value or the extent of his achievement. Professor Leonard
Wolf has said that from the pages of *Dracula*

> there rise images so dreamlike and yet so imperative
> that we experience them as ancient allegories. Every-
> where one looks, there flicker the shadows of primordial
> struggles . . . sex in all its unimaginable innocence, or
> sex reeking with the full perfume of the swamp. And
> all these urgencies are seen or sensed through a hot
> wash of blood, which, deny it though we will, fascinates
> us nearly to the point of shame.[3]

Shame is undoubtedly the appropriate emotion here. The
vampire legend as developed by Stoker is after all born
of sexual frustration and syphilis: it does not fascinate
because it responds to anything in human experience, or
because it tells us anything about the nature of existence:
its appeal derives from its images of murder, exploitation,
necrophilia, sadism, chauvinism and oral sex. Not many
of these are actually the ingredients of a life-enriching
myth. There is nothing the world needs less than a new
vampire story.[4]

4 *Love after Death:*
Henry Rider Haggard

The most impressive of all English writers of occult fiction must on all counts be Henry Rider Haggard. In the first place there is the simple aspect of quantity: the greater part of his enormous literary output, including some thirty-four novels, is composed of stories which either deal directly with the occult, or in which occult interventions play a fundamental part in the evolution of the plot. Moreover the assorted occult aspects can be related to one another as integral parts of a generally consistent if not always coherent philosophy which provided the inspiration for Haggard's own life. He differs in this respect from Stoker, who had no philosophy but was merely haunted by erotic fantasies; from Lovecraft, who never believed in his own myths; and from Dennis Wheatley, who indeed expresses a completely coherent philosophy in his novels, but one which appears to be totally unrelated to everything else in them, and even to everything else about Mr Wheatley himself.

Haggard's incoherence is indeed virtually a source of strength, in the sense that it reflects an attitude to human experience apparently completely free from any kind of dogmatic constraint or preconception. His total relativism is indicated by an entry in his diary made a few months before his death, with reference to the ancient Egyptians:

It is terrific to think that all these hordes were deluded by a faith which we know to be false, as are the multitudes of India and China, by other faiths which we know to be false.... If this inference were true, their lot was terrible indeed. But I for one do not believe it to be true. I look upon religion (from that of the lowest savage up to that of the most advanced Christian) as a ladder stretching from earth to heaven. ... In that ladder the faith of the old Egyptians was a single rung, that which we follow is another rung, and perhaps there are many more, out of our sight and knowledge, for God's skies are far away.[1]

Anyone who holds such a viewpoint is of course free from the inhibitions involved in the orthodox Christian concept that supernatural interventions within the framework of any other religious system were necessarily the work of the Devil, whatever they might seem to be from an objective analysis. Haggard's free-thinking in this area was indeed not approved by his family, his daughter Lilias in particular wondering rather extraordinarily 'how a person so precise in statement, and so severe on others who were not, could allow his judgement wholly to abdicate to his imagination in matters of the spirit'.[2] The truth seems rather that Haggard was simply refusing to let his observation abdicate to the constraints of dogma. It was in any case evident that the whole basis of Haggard's approach to the occult was that precise statements were necessarily inappropriate in an area not subject to the limitations of the physical universe.

This was not the only regard in which Haggard displayed a freedom of approach remarkable in any generation, and exceptionally uncommon in his own. His sympathy for the religious beliefs of other peoples was rendered peculiarly complete and uncomplicated by an almost total absence of any kind of ethnic or racial prejudice. He argues seriously in *Child of Storm* that the civilization of the Zulus is in many ways actually superior in human terms to that of contemporary Europe, which he identifies elsewhere with 'gunpowder, telegraphs, steam, daily newspapers, universal suffrage', which he believes have not only made people not a whit happier but have cursed them with the evils of 'greed, drunkenness, new diseases, gunpowder and general demoralization'. Haggard does indeed tend to dislike the Boers, but this is essentially because of what he regards as their own indefensible attitude towards the blacks. This freedom from prejudice even extends to sexual matters. Haggard appears to accept that miscegenation is impracticable in the white man's world, and the dying black girl Foulata in *King Solomon's Mines* laments that 'the sun may not mate with darkness nor the white the black', but she nonetheless looks forward to finding her lover, John Good R N, eventually in the stars, after death. Good himself complains after his return to England that he 'hadn't seen a woman to touch her, either as regards her figure or the sweetness of her expression'.

Love after death is in fact the continuing theme of Haggard's stories. It is indeed his conviction that love can be found satisfactorily nowhere else. There can be no doubt that at least one motivation for Haggard's concern with the occult was his dissatisfaction with the known world. Young, handsome, physically powerful, popular, intelligent, genial, brilliantly successful, he appears to have accepted by his twenties that the appropriate response to human life was one of despair. He never changed that view. Every allusion he ever made to the subject indicated that he expressed his own sentiments totally in the dying words of Allan Quatermain: 'Well, it is not a good world – nobody can say that it is, save those who wilfully blind themselves to the facts. How can a world be good, in which Money is the moving power,

and Self-interest the guiding star? The wonder is not that
it is so bad, but that there is any good left in it.' This is
not a totally Manichean view. The world is not wholly bad
in itself: there are even aspects of it which make Quatermain reflect that he is glad to have been alive, even though
he also looks forward with great relief to being dead.
There is for example moonlight on the veldt. The rota-
tion of crops and wine-making also get favourable mention in *Barbara Who Came Back*, the story which sets
out most specifically Haggard's views on personal immortality. It is what happens to human relations in the
physical universe that makes it, as Haggard assured
Kipling, ' one of the hells '. The good always suffer at the
hands of the worldly-wise. Love itself may be more of a
curse than a blessing: Haggard noted in his diary that
sex was, 'at any rate in highly civilized conditions, the
source of our worst woes'; and Ayesha explains to Allan
Quatermain that friendship between men and women is
at once a higher and more serviceable relationship than
love, because nothing could be worse than for couples
who had nothing in common except their physical relationship, and were therefore condemned to be bored with
each other's company throughout eternity. But in any
case women may love one for a while, but they have loved
others before, and love is not the whole of their lives:
even the Zulu Mameena, whose love for Quatermain is
unreserved and undying, will do anything for him except
sacrifice her ambition; and Lady Luna Ragnall tells
Quatermain seriously that she would do anything for
him, clearly implying make love to him, but still deceives
him at the end of an occult experiment they conduct together. Nor are ties of gratitude or comradeship to be
counted upon: Heda and Maurice in *Finished* do not
bother to keep in touch with Quatermain, to whom they
owe everything, once they are rich and safe; and Hera,
the wife of Sir Henry Curtis in *Allan Quatermain*, resents

the time her husband spends with the dying Quatermain, who was mortally wounded defending her against her enemies. In what appears to be a deliberate attempt to reach the furthest frontiers of despair, Ayesha grants Quatermain a vision of eternity, in which he attempts to make contact with those he had known and loved on earth, only to discover that he cannot do so, as they were not thinking of him at the time, any more than he had always been thinking of them.

In Haggard's vision, it is the world of physical reality, not that of the occult, in which one encounters true horror. The only hope of human happiness is to be sought in worlds beyond this one, and the first problem is of course to be at all sure that they exist. Haggard in fact did experience a few encounters with the occult in the course of an incredibly busy life, as well as a number of frightening or disturbing experiences which may well have rendered him unusually susceptible in that area. His daughter records that a vicious nanny used to terrify him as a child with 'a disreputable rag doll of particularly hideous aspect, with boot-button eyes, hair of black wool and a sinister leer upon its painted face. . . . Why or how it came to be called She-Who-Must-Be-Obeyed he could not remember but so it was.' The doll certainly provided the name and perhaps some of the eeriness for Haggard's great symbol of the Eternal Feminine, even though there is nothing horrific or sinister in the myth of 'She' as he eventually developed it. He also received an intimation of death in bed one night, when noticing that his hand looked dead in the moonlight and consequently realizing that some day he and it in fact would be dead. The mood of this experience certainly persists in his stories, as one of the most convincing aspects of Allan Quatermain's psychological approach to death is that he fears it while at the same time welcoming it with relief. Haggard also attended Lady Paulet's spiritualist seances in London at

the age of eighteen, but seems to have been generally un-
impressed by them, and not to have found them at all
adequate as an answer to the problems of life and death.
He gave up attending after a few months, writing later
that he believed that the phenomena were unlikely to
have been wholly illusory, but were more likely to have
been the result of the employment of some psychic energy,
'harmful and unwholesome, an unknown force which has
nothing to do with spirits, as we understand them'. It was
the reaction of a man sympathetic, rational, emotionally
uninvolved and above all sensitive to the affronts to
emotions and reason frequently associated with seances.

His African experiences undoubtedly heightened his
interest in the occult by making him acquainted with
tribal myths and practices, but there is no record of his
having undergone any decisive personal experience there.
He had nonetheless become convinced by the time he
married Louise Margitson that he had previously been
incarnated as an ancient Egyptian, a Norseman and a
Zulu and that because of the faults for which he had been
responsible in his previous existences, he was condemned
to bring misfortune to those with whom he became
closely associated this time round.

There are also references in his memoirs to his possession of a faculty for precognition, though without any
corroborating data. However, two experiences later in life
undoubtedly justified his belief in precognition itself and
also in the reality of the curse he felt himself doomed to
bear. In his novel *The Way of the Spirit*, written in 1906,
he depicts the hero, Rupert, hearing nomad musicians,
known as The Wandering Players, who are said by the
Arabs to be ghosts who bring misfortune to all who hear
them, and appear to Rupert before events causing him
great personal suffering. The Egyptian antiquarian, Sir
Gaston Maspero, wrote to Haggard after reading the
book, asking him how he had learned of a legend which

as far as he knew had never been written down before, but which Haggard had described almost exactly in *The Way of the Spirit*. Haggard himself was convinced that he had invented the episode entirely from his imagination. Far more disturbing was the appalling irony of the opening paragraph of *Allan Quatermain*: 'I have just buried my boy, my poor handsome boy of whom I was so proud, and my heart is broken. It is very hard having only one son to lose like this, but God's will be done.' The novel was dedicated to Haggard's own son, Jock. Six years later Jock was dead, and Haggard was haunted for the rest of his life by the emotions which he had attributed to Allan Quatermain, as well as by the reflection that by thus killing off the son of his fictional alter ego, he might somehow have psychically contrived the death of his own son.

There was one other occult experience, which Haggard considered interesting enough to refer to the Society for Psychical Research and to recount in an otherwise singularly unexciting chapter entitled 'Psychical', in his autobiography *The Days of My Life*. He had an unusually vivid nightmare one summer night in 1904, when he dreamed that his black retriever Bob was dying in some brushwood beside water, and was trying by this means to make him aware of its death. It was found later that the dog had been hit that night by a railway train and thrown off a bridge into brushwood by the brink of a river, where it died. The circumstances corresponded exactly to Haggard's dream, of which he told his wife the details when she was awakened by the noise he was making, hours before the fate of the dog was confirmed.

These experiences certainly helped to confirm Haggard's ideas about the occult, and to inspire episodes in some of his fiction. His basic concerns and beliefs seem however to have been formed in his youth, without the aid of any psychic encounters, at a time when he was

living the life of a John Buchan hero. Haggard's despair
over the tragedy of human existence was certainly not
derived from any personal inability to enjoy life. He went
to South Africa at the age of nineteen on the staff of the
lieutenant-governor of Natal, after having studied for the
Foreign Office and fallen in love with a beautiful girl. He
became registrar of the High Court of the Transvaal, as
the youngest head of department in South Africa; made
a most favourable impression on everybody he met as a
genial companion, a good shot and a superb cook; and
fell in love with another beautiful girl. Disappointed in
love again, he reacted in the best romantic tradition by
throwing up his government post and living a 'wild and
reckless' life in Pretoria, which at the time must have
been equivalent to living a wild and reckless life in Dodge
City when the Wild West was at its most exciting and
unhealthy. He then tried his hand at ostrich farming in
the Transvaal; returned to England; and met and married Louise Margitson, who was certainly less strikingly
beautiful than his two previous lost loves. They returned
to Natal just in time for the war of 1881, in which the
Transvaal won its independence. They accordingly
returned to England, where Haggard now began to study
law, as his wife's estate had left him tolerably independent. In the meantime he wrote *Cetewayo and His White
Neighbours*, an indispensable introduction to the history
of South Africa, scrupulously researched and documented
but distinctly coloured by Haggard's admiration for the
Zulus and dislike for the Boers. It was most unsuccessful.
So he turned to fiction, publishing his first novel, *Dawn*,
a few months later. The heroine was interestingly inspired
by the sight of another dazzlingly beautiful girl in the
village church. This effort also failed totally. A second
novel, *The Witch's Head*, was more encouraging in that
its sales reimbursed Haggard for the fifty pounds he had
lost in publishing *Cetewayo* and *Dawn*. A few months

C

later he wrote *King Solomon's Mines* and became the most popular living English author, whose books still outsell those of any of his contemporaries with the exception of Kipling. He also continued his life as adventurer, traveller, farmer and historian, adding massive studies on farming in England, farming in Denmark and the Salvation Army to his output.

One can only wonder that a man sufficiently active in the concerns of this life to have been in his time aspirant diplomat, aspirant lawyer, head of department, judge, Norfolk squire, ostrich farmer, adventurer, historian, agricultural reformer, evangelist for the British Empire and the most successful writer of his age should have found the energy or the inclination to have become so absorbed with the concerns of another level of existence. Haggard could at least claim that he knew what life was about. It qualified him to reflect upon death.

Haggard's occult novels can be conveniently grouped into three categories. There are those which introduce supernatural interventions into tales of high adventure; those which are explicitly moralistic in purpose, serving essentially as vehicles for the expression of Haggard's opinions about life and death; and those in which he develops the enormous symbolic figure of Ayesha, or 'She-Who-Must-Be-Obeyed'.

The first group would include for example *King Solomon's Mines* itself, in which the supernatural element is provided by the demon-witch Gagool, although typically Haggard makes it possible for the reader to believe that Gagool was merely a wicked and deceitful human being; *The Holy Flower*, perfect in construction, suspense and unfailing good humour and incorporating on the occult side precognition and witchcraft; and *The Ivory Child*, possibly Haggard's most successful work in literary terms, rivalling Wilkie Collins' *The Moonstone* for plot, atmosphere, balance and style, but including as an additional bonus hypnotism, telepathy, precognitive dreams, reincarnation, apparitions and a demon elephant. On a marginally lower level of quality if not necessarily of entertainment is *The Treasure of the Lake*, in which the adventure is complicated by the presence of the beautiful 'White Mouse', who loves and rescues Allan Quatermain, without ever leaving him entirely clear as to whether she is black or white, or even whether she is human or a spirit; and *The Ancient Allan*, in which the adventure is presented as an occult exploration by Quatermain and Lady Luna Ragnall, the heroine of *The Ivory Child*. Ironically, the one novel in the Allan Quatermain series, *Allan Quatermain* itself, which has really no occult aspects at all, is the one which has the most significant occult implications for Haggard's own life, in that it contains the reference to the death of Quatermain's son, which anticipated so tragically Haggard's reaction to the death of his own child.

There is perhaps little of an extraordinary nature about these stories, apart from their tremendous if uneven literary skill, and their lack of any of the psychotic undertones of Le Fanu's or Stoker's tales. Haggard indeed never attains the cool perfection of Le Fanu's style, and is often mechanical, repetitive and sloppy. However, he is normally nothing less than a perfect storyteller, with brilliant imagination, an excellent sense of plot, splendid narrative and expository vigour, remarkable humour, effective characterization and a gift for dramatic dialogue which can seriously be compared only with that of Sir Walter Scott at his best. In other words Haggard does not need the assistance of the occult to make his stories interesting.

What adds immensely to the effect of the occult aspects is indeed the cool scepticism with which they are presented, and the manner in which they are almost but not quite explained away. Thus in *The Holy Flower* Quatermain can dismiss his Zulu witchdoctor's forecast of the time at which the mad white man Dogeetah will arrive as merely a guess; but he cannot explain what it was that impelled him to add half an hour to the witchdoctor's estimated time of arrival, and thereby save everybody's lives. Similarly, in *The Ivory Child* the powers of the conjurers Harut and Meerut are dismissed as merely stage-craft, even though nobody is able to explain how the powers of telepathy and hypnotism they possess actually work; but Quatermain is unable even to guess how it was that he and that other infallible shot, Lord Ragnall, could not hit the demon-elephant Jana even at point-blank range, while his Hottentot servant Hans could not miss it.

This is indeed basically technique, although it does in fact correspond to what might be termed the normal run of occult experiences: the occult commonly presents itself as that aspect of an otherwise explicable happening, for which in fact an explanation cannot now be found. Far more important however is what may be termed the atmosphere of Haggard's descriptions of the occult. The events beyond the limits of the physical universe are not presented as symbols of desires either unadmitted or inadmissible, but as simple human experiences on another level of existence. Haggard does not need symbols for his repressions or those of his characters, because he seems to have been incredibly free from the need to repress anything.

It was not only in his attitudes to race that he was singularly immune from the preconceptions which distorted the vision of his contemporaries. His freedom and honesty in sexual matters are also literally unique. For example he does not seem to have been bothered by three issues unmentioned elsewhere in respectable Victorian or Edwardian fiction: pornography, lesbianism and female nudity. Quatermain observes in *Finished* that Dr Rodd's library contains 'novels, mostly French, and other volumes of a sort that I imagine are generally kept under lock and key'. In the same novel, the European heroine Heda asks Quatermain: 'Tell me, Mr Quatermain, is it possible for one woman to be in love with another?' Quatermain replies with what he calls the 'cheap joke' that 'women, as far as I had observed them, were generally in love either with a man or with themselves, perhaps more often with the latter than the former'. However, he questions the female witchdoctor Nombe, and learns that all men are hateful to her and that she will never be parted from Heda as long as she lives. Quatermain describes her feelings at the time as abnormal and unnatural. He nonetheless describes as 'splendid' and 'triumphant' the death in which Nombe gives her life for Heda, dying with the words: 'Sister, forget me not, Sister, who will await you for a thousand years.'

In *Allan's Wife*, Quatermain's own wife Stella is the object of passionate love by the baboon-woman Hendrijka, who tells Quatermain that 'they say in the kralls that men love women better than women love women. But it is a lie.' Quatermain does not condemn her attitude, commenting merely that it 'is generally supposed that this passion only exists in strength when the object is of another sex from the lover, but I confess that, both in this instance and in some others which I have met with, this has not been my experience'. The statement is hardly revolutionary or even very well expressed, but it stands alone in the popular fiction of its time.

Haggard's success in creating female archetypes is certainly consistent with his unfailing capacity to confront the supreme physical fact of female nudity without the complications of prudery or prurience. Nudity occurs in his stories probably more often than it does in those of Dennis Wheatley, for example. Mameena is normally naked, except for her apron of blue beads, and she is even divested of that in *Child of Storm*; Ayesha, who dresses in transparent robes when she is dressed, strips before Kallikrates and Amentares in *Wisdom's Daughter*; and the two queens in *Allan Quatermain* are specifically described in the narrative as wearing robes that left their breasts uncovered. This was too much for Haggard's illustrators, who invariably felt compelled to cover the ladies up. However, the only emotions ever attributed to the observers of any of these displays are wonder and admiration. Quatermain, lying on his couch, watches the statuesque and naked Mameena departing from his hut on hands and knees with only the comment: 'She could even *crawl* gracefully!' Haggard presents his women as objects of literally unbounded love, but never as sex objects.

While Haggard did not find it necessary to transform his women into vampires in order to convey the fact that they loved and even desired each other, he did portray them as essentially spirits. There is no doubt that Haggard's heroines play far more important and active roles when they are out of their bodies than when they are in them. White Mouse in *The Treasure of the Lake*, for example, can only be assumed to be a spirit, even though she never admits this directly to Quatermain, whom she loves, telling him that there is really no important difference between women and spirits anyway. Lady Luna Ragnall and Quatermain console themselves for their inability to marry in their present existence by reliving previous existences in which they had been lovers. The heroine of *Barbara Who Came Back* dies, is reunited on the astral plane with all who had loved her and preceded her in death, including her dog, but eventually decides to allow herself to be reincarnated into the physical world she has learned to regard with horror, in order to assist the spiritual development of others still unlucky enough to be alive.

But the spiritual activities of all these ladies are limited and sedate compared with those of Haggard's archetypal creation, the beautiful Mameena, who quite literally haunts his three other great adventure stories, *Marie*, *Child of Storm* and *Finished*, and plays while still dead a decisive role in *The Ivory Child*. Her earthly life is indeed sufficiently energetic: she pretends to royal blood to which she has no claim; she seduces Saduko, chief of the Amangwane, into massacring another tribe to acquire the bride-price to marry her, but actually marries the objectionable and repulsive Masupo, chief of the Amansomi. She then establishes an adulterous relationship with Saduko, who has in the meantime married the good and noble Nandie, princess of the Zulu house of Senzagakona; she poisons their child in order to have Masupo executed for the murder, and becomes Saduko's second wife, only to betray him for Umbelazi, the crown prince of the Senzagakonas, whom Saduko in revenge leaves to be killed by Cetewayo. Finally she poisons herself in order to escape execution for her crimes. Mameeka also loves Quatermain, whom she kisses, living and dead, and becomes the first heroine in respectable English fiction to take her moocha off in public, when she is stripped and examined during one of her trials.

However, her career is even more dramatic after death. Her spirit appears repeatedly to Quatermain, although he is at the time unsure whether it is actually her or the almost equally beautiful Nombe. She embraces him at least once, although he is not wholly sure at the time whether he actually felt her or not; she protects him from a demon-elephant; she rides before him to frighten off the Zulus while he escapes from the field of Isandlhwana. She taunts the unfortunate Saduko on his death-bed, terrorizes Nombe for plotting against Quatermain's life, and abuses the spirits of Quatermain's two dead wives for having become too ethereal to be able to love him properly when the time comes for him to rejoin them all. Similarly she abuses Quatermain's servant Hans, when his

spirit encounters hers in a dream, for failing to give her
the royal salute to which she had no legitimate claim during her earthly life; and she is in fact portrayed in a
magnificent passage as enjoying after death the imperial
homage which she had sought as a living woman by way
of adultery, child-murder, high treason and war:

> At last I got out of that quiet place and among
> mountains where were dark kloofs, and there among
> the kloofs I heard Zulu impis singing their war-song;
> yes, they sang the *ingoma* or something very like it. Now
> suddenly in a pass of the mountains along which I sped,
> there appeared before me a very beautiful woman
> whose skin shone like the best copper coffee kettle after
> I have polished it, Baas. She was dressed in a leopard-
> like moocha and wore on her shoulders a fur kaross,
> and about her neck a circlet of blue beads, and from
> her hair there rose one crane's feather tall as a walking-
> stick, and in her hand she held a little spear. No flowers
> sprang beneath her feet when she walked towards me,
> and no birds sang, only the air was filled with the sound
> of a royal salute which rolled among the mountains like
> the roar of thunder, and her eyes flashed like summer
> lightning.

It is certainly remarkable that there is no suggestion
at all that Mameena has undergone any punishment or
even any remorse for actions which would entitle her to
rank among the most formidable villainesses of fiction. It
is of course possible that Haggard, as a believer in reincarnation, assumes that our crimes and follies are expiated
in subsequent existences on an earth which he regards as
a hell. It is at least evident that he never bothered to
formulate a rigid system of moral values. His attitude
remained that of Allan Quatermain in *Finished*:

> Our lives cannot be judged by our deeds; they must

be judged by our desires or rather by our moral attitude
... those who seek to climb out of the pit, those who
strive, however vainly, to fashion failure to success,
are, by comparison, the righteous, while those who are
content to wallow in our native mire and to glut themselves with the daily bread of vice, are the unrighteous.'

It leaves a great deal of room for interpretation, which is
no doubt exactly what Haggard intended. His position
remained flexible to the end. Adverse comments on the
morality of his novel *Beatrice* indeed worried him to the
extent that he insisted that the last paragraph of the book
should be shown on the screen before each cinema per-
formance of the story, so that the audience might learn
that: 'Whatever the excuse or temptation, the man or
woman who falls into undesirable relation with a married
member of the other sex is both a sinner and a fool, and
in this coin or that, will certainly be called upon to pay
the price of sin and folly.' On the other hand, he also
noted privately in his diary that 'perhaps, in its day, for
ends whereof we know nothing, the flesh was meant to be
our master to rule as the spirit shall rule in its appointed
kingdom. Who can say?' It was a possibility worth con-
sidering, and Haggard was prepared to leave it at that.
He had other things to think about.

One of the things which he continued to think about all
his life was the presentation in fiction of perhaps the
ultimate female archetype, the Queen of the Heavens,
whose cult had existed throughout the Middle Ages,
among the Egyptians, the modern African tribes, the
ancient Germans, the Celts and the Ainu of Japan. The
'She-Who-Must-Be-Obeyed' quartet, *She, Ayesha, She
and Allan* and *Wisdom's Daughter* constitute Haggard's
quite deliberate though distinctly tentative foray into
genuine myth-making and the world of symbolism. The
occult elements in his other books are presented as aspects

of reality, as has been said; Luna Ragnall, White Mouse and even Mameena are all mortal in some respects, even though, especially in the case of Mameena, possessed of literally immortal beauty, passion and will; She or Ayesha, to use her more euphonious alternative name, is not mortal and presumably never has been. In terms of Haggard's own thinking, of course, this may not really matter: if we all are, even when physically existent, merely embodied spirits, the distinction between the mortal and the immortal becomes very tenuous indeed. This is indeed one of the numerous problems with which Haggard found himself compelled to grapple when composing his giant myth. They were never resolved satisfactorily. If they could have been, there would have been no need of a myth.

There is at least no doubt that Ayesha is a different category of being from that of human life. She appears first as the veiled queen of an African tribe inhabiting the hidden city of Kor. She explains to the two British explorers who are brought before her that she has been living there for two thousand years, awaiting the return of her lover Kallikrates, whose death she had in fact been responsible for when he was a priest of Isis in ancient Egypt. As in the case of Mameena, Haggard is not particularly concerned with the crimes of his female archetypes. One of the Englishmen, Leo Vincy, is recognized by Ayesha as the reincarnation of Kallikrates, from whom he had previously discovered himself to be descended. After many adventures and more bloodshed, Ayesha leads Vincy to bathe in the legendary Pillar of Fire, which is also the Pillar of Life in order that he might become immortal with her. She bathes first herself, to allay his fears, but is consumed by the flames and shrivels to ashes, leaving Vincy and his absurdly-named mentor Holly totally at a loss.

So was the author. Haggard had many reasons for feeling less than satisfied with his first venture into myth-making. In the first place, it is much less successful as a story than the Quatermain tales, because the characters of Vincy and Holly are quite uninteresting and unconvincing. Ayesha herself is abundantly interesting and even convincing, but also baffling. She is in fact a superbly comprehensive evocation of the Eternal Feminine, but she is utterly elusive both as a personality and even as a being. She is ruthless, fascinating, incomparably beautiful, capricious and omnipotent in her dealing with mortals of the human species. However, her own immortality is in some sense conditional since it was necessary for her to bathe in the Pillar of Fire to acquire her first two thousand years of existence in the physical world, and her second attempt causes her own physical destruction. She is therefore something less than a goddess in the usual sense, and indeed refers to herself as being bound by the Eternal Law. She might well stand for a symbol of ideal beauty, which can neither exist permanently in the physical universe nor be united with humanity there, were it not for the fact that her own personality seems somewhat less than ideal. On the other hand, she is not simply a siren, destroying herself rather than luring mortals to destruction.

Haggard was himself fully aware of the fact that his treatment of the Ayesha myth had not been wholly satisfactory. He was also aware of its importance: Kipling wrote, assuring him that 'anything any of us did well was no credit to us ... it came from somewhere else ... we were, in fact, only telephone wires.... You did not write *She*, you know, something wrote it through you!'[3] Obviously, the wires were not clear at the time, and the something that wrote *She* should be allowed a second try. This presented no technical difficulty: as Haggard told W. H. Pollock, 'What is there to prevent her immediate reincarnation, in Tibet, let us say?'[4] The only real surprise is that Haggard waited some eighteen years before buckling to the task again. *Ayesha* returned in the book of that name, published in 1905. 'The appointed years – alas! how many of them – are gone by,' he told Andrew Lang, 'leaving Ayesha lovely and loving and ourselves alive.... To you therefore who accepted the first, I offer this further history of one of the various incarnations of that Immortal.' At the same time, he informed his readers that:

> Not with a view of conciliating those readers who on principle object to sequels, but as a matter of fact, the Author wish to say that he does not so regard this book. Rather does he venture to ask that it should be considered as the conclusion of an imaginative tragedy (if he may so call it) whereof one half has been already published.

The distinction is hardly clear, but there is at least no doubt that the return of Ayesha adds some interesting and philosophically valid new dimensions to the myth, even though it also adds some new problems. Ayesha is indeed reincarnated in the neighbourhood of Tibet, where she reigns again on earth. She again summons Vincy and Holly to her, where as before they find her veiled. This however is now because the body in which she walks the earth is hideously charred and burned by the Pillar of Fire. Her original body was of course not disfigured but reduced to ashes, so the mechanics of her incarnation are not entirely clear. Its symbolic significance is however revealed when Ayesha disrobes to reveal her physical destruction in response to a challenge from the beautiful if mortal Atene, who is her rival for the love of Vincy. This act of supreme humiliation and honesty causes Ayesha's own body to be restored to its original superhuman beauty. Atene then leads a revolution against Ayesha; Vincy and Holly lead Ayesha's armies in one of the furious pitched battles which Haggard never wearied of describing and their victory is gained when Ayesha looses hurricanes and lightning upon the rebels. Atene kills herself, and Vincy claims Ayesha as his bride. She is however still some order of goddess and Vincy only mortal, and Vincy dies in her embrace, falling upon the dead body of Atene, who had promised to prepare the path for him to tread, and make ready his place in the Underworld. Ayesha then simply vanishes, later reappearing to the dying Holly, who rushes from his deathbed to be with her in some other world.

Haggard's literary technique is perhaps hardly more successful in *Ayesha* than it had been in *She*, because of the intrinsic impossibility of making Vincy and Holly convincing or even interesting. The myth however gains tremendously in its second instalment. The transformation of Ayesha's destroyed body symbolizes the recreative powers of love and truth, and the death of Vincy reminds us that complete union with ideal beauty cannot be attained within the limits of the physical universe. It is necessary that time and space should be transcended, and this can be accomplished only by the act of dying. There are on the other hand some aspects which do not resolve themselves so effectively. The conflict between Ayesha and Atene is presented as a version of the duel between sacred and profane love. However, Ayesha's love is not simply spiritual, since it involves physical union with Vincy; and Atene's love is not simply physical, since she looks forward to reunion with Vincy in a world beyond death. There is also a clear implication that Ayesha herself regards her relationship with Holly as being more important and more permanent than her love for Vincy. In any case, the distinction between Ayesha and Atene is not even that between beauty which uplifts and beauty which degrades: if Atene is disloyal, Ayesha is a murderess; both are liars; and Ayesha's love has the effect of destroying Vincy, physically at least, while Atene's love destroys herself. Moreover, if Ayesha can look forward to recovering Vincy after death, so apparently can Atene.

Least of all does Ayesha solve the basic problem of who or what she actually is. A priest at the end of the book refers to her as ' the woman – or the sorceress – or the mighty evil spirit...' all of which descriptions are in fact evidently inadequate. It does however seem inherent in Haggard's conception that Ayesha should in fact remain equivocal and ill-defined: the most authentic aspect of Haggard's whole attitude towards the occult is that there is no point in trying to be precise when dealing with matters which by their nature cannot be fully comprehended by the denizens of a physical universe. It is in any case not inappropriate that a symbol of the Eternal Feminine should be all things to all men, and different things to the same man.

This quality of infinite variety is indeed emphasized in the third volume of the Ayesha quartet, *She and Allan*, published sixteen years after *Ayesha*, but in fact presented as an introduction to *She*, which precedes it by thirty-four years. Like all the Quatermain stories, the book is first of all a superb adventure story of Africa, written with all the skill of a man who would certainly appear to be the best writer of adventure stories in the language. It is also at least a partially successful attempt by Haggard to bring together his three great archetypes, Ayesha, Mameena and Quatermain himself. It is in *She and Allan* that Quatermain is treated by Ayesha to the vision of the afterlife in which he makes the despairing discovery that his two dead wives had literally forgotten about him, as they had forgotten other affairs of the earth. So had his parents and his friends. The only person who remembered him was in fact Mameena because, as she explains to him, she was 'still a sinful woman with a woman's love and of the earth, earthy'. In case this might comfort him at all, Ayesha asks if it was 'really thy desire to pass from the

gentle, ordered claspings of those white souls' who had
forgotten him 'to the tumultuous arms of such a one as
this'. Life was not meant to be easy. Neither was death.

Ayesha does at least make some reasonably definite
statements about her own nature to Quatermain. She is
the Eternal Feminine; she is a goddess, albeit with limited
powers, subject to the Law of Nature; she is Woman
Incarnate; she is also Nature Incarnate, revealed in the
feminine form of humanity, which means that she is either
the Goddess Isis or spiritually linked with her. It is however still fundamental to the validity of the myth that its
nature should never be wholly clarified, and Ayesha is left
endowed with some traits which seem to be inconsistent
with spiritual perfection. For a start, she gets on Quatermain's nerves: he is convinced that two thousand years
of immortality would have no attractions for him if it
meant that he had to listen to Ayesha rating him for much
of the time. He indeed generally regards her, as does his
ferocious Zulu companion Unslopogaas, as a witch
deceitful and capricious. The old Zulu witchdoctor
Zikali, who himself is more than human, sees her also as a
witch, but a witch whose function is to reveal truth to
mankind. There is no final answer.

Nor is there a satisfactory final answer in the last of
the Ayesha stories, Ayesha's own memoir of her birth and
her first incarnation, *Wisdom's Daughter*. Ayesha tells
us that she is the daughter of Isis, who is Nature, and
whose powers she shares to some extent. She also says
that Isis herself may be only a parable or myth, and
Ayesha's actual birth is undoubtedly human. Her purpose
on earth is apparently to struggle with Aphrodite, who
symbolizes Life, but whose effect on humanity is to render
it forgetful of the things of the spirit. Again, the issue
would seem to be one of sacred and profane love, were
it not for the fact that some of Ayesha's own activities are
more than somewhat profane. She destroys Sidon,

organizes the murder of King Tenes, kills King Ochus, indulges schemes of military conquest and finally kills her beloved Kallikrates when he embraces Amentaras, the incarnation of Aphrodite, who is to be reincarnated two thousand years later as Atene. This is apparently unimportant, however, as Ayesha reflects that: 'From the flesh came my sins, because it was begotten of other flesh and the flesh is sin incarnate. Yet my soul sins not, because it comes from that which is sinless and ... to this holy fount at last it shall return again.' The holy fount is of course Isis, 'a beauteous symbol with a hidden face ruling o'er the world ... formless, yet in every form, dead, yet living in all that breathes, a priest-bred phantasy, yet the one great truth,' but herself only 'one of Divinity's thousand forms'.

These are massive problems to encounter in what are presented as basically tales of adventure. They are certainly dealt with by Haggard far more acceptably in the medium of the adventure yarn, however, than in his explicitly moral stories, *The Way of the Spirit, Love Eternal, Beatrice* and *Barbara Who Came Back*, which are interesting only to the extent that they express Haggard's views of the occult. Apart from that, they are in general mawkish, uninspired, contrived and profoundly unentertaining. The fact is that Haggard found an ideal form of expression in the story of African adventure, and in six or seven novels of this genre he stands supreme both as storyteller and myth-maker. Nor are his myths simply symbols of sexual variations. He is concerned with the same order of human problems as Plato was, with the issues of immortality, the varying roles of flesh and spirit, expiation, retribution and love. All this is worlds away from Cthulhu, Dracula and their ilk.

5 The Myth that Never was: Howard P. Lovecraft

While Bram Stoker was on every count the most unlikely producer of stories of the occult, Lovecraft could hardly have been anything else. Stoker was normal to the point of highly proficient mediocrity: athletic, genial, vastly sociable, a man of affairs, an ideal private secretary, distinguished intellectually only for his incredible industry in dealing with correspondence of a strictly business nature. He was indeed a natural writer of adolescent adventure stories who happened by sheer accident to catch a sado-erotic legend in flight and send it winging through uninterrupted reprintings. Nothing of this applies to Lovecraft. All that he shares with Stoker and the other writers discussed here is the reputation of a myth-maker and the honour of being among the most enthusiastically plagiarized of storytellers.

Howard Phillips Lovecraft was born in Providence, Rhode Island in 1890, and died there, forty-seven years later. His life displayed an uninterrupted pattern of social inadequacy, far more so than that of his purported literary ancestor, Edgar Allan Poe. Poe at least was handsome, frequently popular, disastrously sociable and happily if tragically married. He also surprisingly attained the rank of regimental sergeant-major in the United States Army at the age of nineteen, which indicates an undoubted capacity for ordered and extrovert behaviour. Lovecraft could never have been one of nature's N C OS.

His father died insane, possibly of syphilis, when he was only nine, after spending five years in a mental institution. His mother was by all accounts intensely neurotic, obsessed with ample justification with financial worries, and totally indulgent, allowing Lovecraft to stuff himself unrestrainedly with ice-cream and to go to bed and get up entirely as he wished. More ominously, she treated him as far as possible as a girl until the age of six, dressing him invariably in Little Lord Fauntleroy suits. Lovecraft was withdrawn from school at the age of nine, after a breakdown involving nervous disorders, digestive troubles, migraines and kidney ailments. He grew up to add to these the peculiarly unusual complaint of poikilothermism, the chief characteristic of which is that the body 'loses the normal mammalian ability' to keep its 'temperature constant, regardless of changes in the ambient temperature'. Instead, it 'assumes the temperature of its surroundings', as if one were a reptile or a fish.[1] It is at least reasonable to imagine that this physical condition may largely have explained Lovecraft's obsession with images of unnatural or more accurately supernatural miscegenation, as a result of which mongrel species emerge, possessing both human and reptilian or piscine features, seen in stories such as *The Shadow Over Innsmouth* and, of course, *Dagon*. It undoubtedly helped to influence Lovecraft's unusual mode of living. Since he could be comfortable only when the temperature was over eighty degrees fahrenheit, he was virtually compelled to stay indoors all through the North American winter. He had also developed through his mother's indulgence a preference for working and reading all night, and either sleeping during the day, or continuing to study by artificial light with the blinds drawn. The end result was that Lovecraft was wont to stir outside only after dark, on summer nights, like a character from one of his own stories.

He also looked like one. Physically he was tall, with a body weight ranging remarkably from over 200 pounds, when his wife was feeding him, to around 145 when he followed his own preferences in food. He had a long head and gaunt, irregular features, totally unattractive if not precisely ugly. His nocturnal habits and repellent physical appearance would have encouraged him to adopt a solitary life, even apart from his comprehensive range of obsessional hatreds. These included all forms of alcohol: 'beer feeds the sensual and beastly nature ... I can't see that it does much save coarsen, animalize and degrade ... I am nauseated by even the distant stink of any alcoholic liquor'; tobacco: 'to me the ultimate horror on earth is a smoking car'; seafood and salt water generally: 'I have hated fish and feared the sea and everything connected with it since I was two years old'; dogs: 'noisy, smelly, pawing, slobbering, messy ... panting, wheezing, fumbling, drooling'; motion pictures: 'suited to the grovelling taste of the mindless and promiscuous rabble'; Jews: 'beady-eyed, rat-faced Asiatics'; Irish: 'a mongrel mass of ignorance and crime and superstition'; Czechs: 'depraved beasts, harpies, decayed physically and spiritually'; and the lower orders in general: 'a bastard mess of stewing mongrel flesh without intellect, repellent to eye, nose and imagination'. On the other hand, he appears to have liked cats: 'gentlemen and the pets of gentlemen', and the Aryan race: 'the maintenance of civilization rests today with that magnificent Teutonic stock.... The Teuton is the summit of evolution'. Surprisingly enough, although he seems to have been without even a casual interest in sex, on his wife's testimony, he was 'an adequately excellent lover' who could indeed 'perform'.[2]

Sprague de Camp attributes to Lovecraft 'keen intelligence, vast knowledge, artistic sensitivity, strict personal probity, charm, courtesy and kindness'. If he indeed possessed these qualities, one can only note the extraordinary divergence between the man and his principles. The fact is that Lovecraft's expressed views on race and culture would have been judged immoderate in Nazi Germany. It is of course true that one may possess great artistic ability along with perverse and psychopathic views on society. On the other hand, it is peculiarly hard to preserve this dichotomy in literature, as the literary artist works essentially with problems of human experience and personality, and is therefore necessarily disadvantaged if he has in fact shared few human experiences and hates most human beings. Moreover, Lovecraft's claim to be taken seriously as a myth-maker would necessarily depend to a peculiar degree on the extent to which his particular myth responds to genuine human concerns, and on the sheer technical skill with which he develops it. Lovecraft himself had no doubts about the relevance and consistency of his myth: ' All my stories, unconnected as they may be, are based on the fundamental lore or legend that this world was inhabited at one time by another race, who, in practising black magic, lost their foothold and were expelled, yet live on outside ever ready to take possession of this earth again.' The notion is not a bizarre one, and indeed seems to grow in plausibility as increasing note is taken of phenomena which certainly suggest that previous cultures possessed skills immensely superior to their presumed levels of technology. Books have been written and fortunes made elaborating the possibility that astronauts from the stars might have visited the earth and left some of their constructions behind, or at least trained the local inhabitants in some of their skills. This is not however Lovecraft's particular concern. In any case, as an unflinchingly materialistic atheist, Lovecraft did not believe a word of his own myths, or anybody else's.

Lovecraft's concern is entirely with manufactured

horrors. An effective writer of science-fiction must have some acquaintance with basic scientific principles if he is not to spoil his best effects with technical absurdities; a maker of myths must have some sympathy for genuine human hopes and fears if his myths are to evoke any emotional response from his readers. Lovecraft was as deficient in technical expertise of any kind as he was in the understanding of the human predicament.

Three main themes emerge from his writings. There is first of all the theme of miscegenation – presumably reflecting Lovecraft's loathing for all manner of men except the Anglo-Saxon protestants of whom he was himself hardly a successful exemplar – in which typically New England seaports are overrun by the products of mis-matings between Yankee sailormen and assorted beasts of the sea and water, including, oddly enough, frogs. Love-craft may not have been sufficiently interested in repro–ductive processes to have been aware of the fact that there was just no way in which even the most desperate Yankee sailorman could have impregnated a fish, or vice versa. More likely, he simply did not care about such technicali-ties. Secondly, there is the theme of the ghoul, which again is singularly lacking in any kind of message for the human race: nobody is really interested in whether or not supernatural, bat-winged hounds dine off the bodies of the dead in cemeteries at night. They don't, of course, but it would really make very little difference to anybody if they did. Finally, there is what has come to be extravagantly known as the 'Cthulhu Mythos'.

There are several angles to the Cthulhu concept. There is a mad Arab, Abdul Azred, the author of a terrifying work called the *Necronomicon*, all about 'nameless aeons and inconceivable dimensions to worlds of elder, outer entity', of which unfortunately Lovecraft quotes only the one dreary couplet:

> That is not dead which can eternal lie,
> And with strange eons even death may die.

The subject of this poetical effort is indeed Cthulhu himself, gelatinous, enormous, equipped with claws, bats' wings and tentacles growing out of his head, who sleeps under the Pacific in his house in the cyclopean city of R'lyeh. From time to time he is incautiously awakened, and then there is indeed hell to pay. Cthulhu originally came from the stars, along with his relations Yuggoth, Tsathoggua, Yog-Sothoth *et al*, or alternatively they might have come from Pluto, in the name of which Lovecraft sees the most gratifying implications. Since Lovecraft's idea seems to be that these and other Great Old Ones actually flew with wings, like bats, from wherever they came from to here, the actual point of origin hardly matters: as one cannot fly with wings in space, they would never have made the trip anyway. And finally there are unwise researchers in the arcane, who are forever finding evidence in the Miskatonic University at Arkham, Massachusetts, which puts them on the track of the Old Ones, who are apparently conscious enough to take steps themselves to deal with these snoopers.

The definitive stories of the Cthulhu Mythos are *The Call of Cthulhu* and *At The Mountains of Madness*, both published in 1927, and *The Haunter of the Dark*, published nine years later. Together, it might be said, they tell one more about Cthulhu than most people would want to know. Cthulhu himself is introduced in *The Call of Cthulhu*, which is in fact a succinct and well-constructed story, told with far more restraint than Lovecraft normally exercised. Cthulhu appears first as a statue,

> representing a monster, of a form which only a diseased fancy could conceive. If I say that my somewhat extravagant imagination yielded simultaneous pictures of an octopus, a dragon and a human caricature, I shall

not be unfaithful to the spirit of the thing. A pulpy, ten-tacled head surmounted a grotesque and scaly body with rudimentary wings....

The monster is found to be worshipped in the precincts of New Orleans by adorers who reiterate the sacred formula '*Ph'nglui mglw'nafh Cthulhu R'lyeh wgah'nagl fhtagn*', which of course means 'In his house at R'lyeh great Cthulhu lies dreaming'. The city of R'lyeh is subsequently found by unfortunate sailors in the South Pacific, 'built in measureless eons behind history by the vast, loathsome shapes that seeped down from the dark stars ... the geometry of the place ... was abnormal, non-Euclidean and loathsomely redolent of spheres and dimensions apart from ours'.[3] The city, this time located in the South Pole, is described with greater lavishness in *At the Mountains of Madness*:

> A Cyclopean city of no architecture known to man or to human imagination, with vast aggregations of night-black masonry embodying monstrous perversions of geometrical laws. There were truncated cones, some-times terraced or fluted, surmounted by tall cylindrical shafts here and there bulbously enlarged and often capped with tiers of thinnish scalloped discs; and strange beetling table-like constructions suggesting piles of multitudinous rectangular slabs or circular plates or five-pointed stars....

The overall effect is none too clear. It does however make the narrator think

> again of the eldritch [Lovecraft's favourite adjective] primal myths that had so persistently haunted me since my first sight of this dead Antarctic world – of the demoniac plateau of Leng, of the Mi-Go, or abominable Snow Men of the Himalayas, of the Pnakotic Manuscripts with their prehuman implications, of the

Cthulhu cult, of the *Necronomicon,* and of the Hyperborean legends of formless Tsathoggua and the worse than formless star spawn associated with that semi-entity.

Gibberish is in fact Lovecraft's strongest point: as the tale drags tediously on, we are treated to a vision of 'a megalopolis ranking with such whispered prehuman blasphemies as Valusia, R'lyeh, Ib in the land of Mnar and the Nameless City of Arabia Deserta'. Roughly speaking all this is the work of the Old Ones, who had been 'able to traverse the interstellar ether on their vast membraneous wings. . . . They lived under the sea a good deal, building fantastic cities and fighting terrific battles with nameless adversaries by means of intricate devices employing unknown principles of energy'. Their mistake was to create a race of servants called 'Shoggoths', 'multicellular protoplasmic masses capable of molding their tissues into all sorts of temporary organs under hypnotic influence and thereby forming ideal slaves to perform the heavy work of the community'. These Shoggoths, 'viscous agglutinations of bubbling cells – rubbery fifteen-foot spheroids infinitely plastic and ductile', eventually revolt against the Old Ones, who are driven back to the sea, until they win a complete victory against the Shoggoths, employing 'curious weapons of molecular and atomic disturbance against the rebel entities. . . . And so on and so on.

The Haunter of the Dark adds a final element of self-indulgence: Lovecraft, in addition to repeating his usual catalogue of invented books or place-names to give verisimilitude to his contrived dream-world, has as hero a writer of occult fiction, obviously very like himself, living in Providence, Rhode Island, where he lived, and publishing stories the names of which echo Lovecraft's own. It is incidentally symptomatic of Lovecraft's relentless straining for effect that he describes colonial New England towns in language appropriate for apparitions of positively neolithic ancestry: 'He would train his field-glasses on that spectral, unreachable world beyond the curling smoke.... Even with optical aid Federal Hill seemed somehow alien, half-fabulous and linked to the unreal, intangible marvels of Blake's own tales and pictures. The feeling would persist long after the hill had faded into the violet, lamp-starred twilight, and the courthouse floodlights and the red Industrial Trust beacon had blazed up to make the night grotesque.' Providence was never like this.

Blake at last goes over the edge: he thinks upon 'the ancient legends of Ultimate Chaos, at whose centre sprawls the blind idiot god Azathoth, Lord of All Things, encircled by his flopping horde of mindless and amorphous dancers, and lulled by the thin monotonous piping of a demoniac flute held in nameless paws'. At last he realizes that what he fears is 'an avatar of Nyarlathotep, who in antique and shadowy Khem even took the form of man. I remember Yuggoth, and more distant Shaggai and the ultimate void of the black planets', and departs to his origins with the soul-searing cry of 'Ia ... ngai ... ygg'. It was one way to go.

There is no denying that Lovecraft has considerable narrative skill when he exercises any kind of self-restraint, as he does only in the shorter stories like *The Call of Cthulhu*; a considerable vocabulary, heavily weighted on the polysyllabic side; and considerable though severely limited imaginative vision. His faults encompass every imaginable literary sin. His admirers interestingly tend to regard these failings as almost a positive virtue: for example his biographer and fellow aficionado of the occult, Sprague de Camp asserts that 'the essential quality of a good storyteller is neither accurate observation, nor warm human sympathy, nor technical polish, nor ingenuity in plotting, helpful as all these may be. It is a certain vividness of imagination, enabling the writer to grip the reader's attention and sustain it to the end. This Lovecraft had.' Indeed, de Camp suggests that Lovecraft 'stands on a level with Poe or even a shade above.... He exerted wide influence among writers in his genre. He turned out spine-chilling tales that provide first-rate entertainment; and that, after all, is the prime test of any popular fiction.'⁴ This is an arguable point of view, but it is hardly adequate support for ranking Lovecraft above Poe in any hierarchy of literary merit. There is no doubt that the comparison can hardly be avoided, because Lovecraft himself was obsessed with the thought of Poe as inspirator and exemplar. He first encountered the great American at the age of eight, on his own account: 'I struck EDGAR ALLAN POE! It was my downfall, and . . . I saw the blue firmament of Argos and Sicily darkened by the miasmal exhalations of his tomb!'⁵ Poe, according to de Camp, 'remained his lifelong enthusiasm and the strongest single influence upon him'. De Camp even suggests that Lovecraft 'entertained an illusion of romantics like Poe, that the true artistic genius was too pure of soul and too delicate of sensibility, to need, or even to tolerate, the discipline of learning mere technique'.

If this in fact is what Lovecraft thought Poe believed, one is justified in asserting that Lovecraft never understood anything about Poe, and can indeed scarcely have read him with any attention. Poe was in fact the most rigorously disciplined of technicians, who unflaggingly applied to his own work his own dictum that 'the sequel to inspiration has to be the patient, systematic, intensive application of the intelligence.' Vincent Buranelli in fact claims that 'there has never been a more disciplined artist [than Poe].... His industry was monumental, his dissatisfaction with inferior work implacable.'⁶ Nor was this rigid

self-discipline in any way alien to Poe's natural temperament: the man who could earn the praise of his superior
officer for the manner in which he performed the duties
of company clerk and assistant in the subsistent department of the 1st Regiment of Artillery, United States
Army, was certainly not temperamentally indisposed to
punctuality and routine. It is wholly typical of Lovecraft's
tragically distorted view of life that he should have taken
Poe's occasional weaknesses for his strengths, his lapses for
his achievement. The thought that Lovecraft could have
regarded himself as his spiritual and literary heir would
have been enough to make Poe turn in his grave. Edmund
Wilson has put the case with characteristic succinctness:
'The fact that [Lovecraft's] verbose and undistinguished
style has been compared to Poe's is only one of the many
sad signs that almost nobody any more pays any real
attention to writing.' Lovecraft's only real contribution to
literature might indeed be to serve as a contrast to Poe,
illustrating the difference between discipline and indisci-
pline, between genius and obsession, between genuine
myth-making and contrived exercises in unconvincing
horror.

Lovecraft is in fact an essentially tragic and ineffectual
figure, possessed by virtually insane prejudices, and almost
totally alienated from human sympathies or human
experience, who contrived with the aid of a limited
imagination to construct thoroughly artificial images
intended to be horrific, but lacking any element of physical or psychological credibility to make them convincing. The fact that it is still possible to talk of a Cthulhu
Mythos at all is due far less to Lovecraft's own efforts,
than to those of three men without whose interested
endeavours Lovecraft himself would be most unlikely
ever to have achieved republication.

The Cthulhu Mythos exists in the first place because
two of Lovecraft's acquaintances, August Derleth and

Donald Wandrei, chose to pretend that it existed. Both wrote stories after Lovecraft's death, employing the Cthulhu theme. Derleth indeed founded a publishing company, Arkham House, mainly to publish Lovecraft's stories, as well as his own and Wandrei's. Lovecraft's close friend Clark Ashton Smith, the highly talented American Robert Bloch and the Englishman Brian Lumley also began to write Cthulhu stories. And so, most importantly, did Colin Wilson.

It was hardly a case of love at first sight between Wilson and Lovecraft. In his study of fantasy, *The Strength to Dream*, Wilson described Lovecraft very truthfully as 'an atrocious writer', who 'began as one of the worst and most florid writers of the twentieth century', but who, although he was 'such a bad writer ... has some of the same kind of importance as Kafka. If his work fails as literature, it still holds an interest as a psychological case-history.' This argument could really be sustained, of course, only if it could be shown that Lovecraft's myths and symbols were of anything like the same relevance as Kafka's to the human situation. Wilson tries to prove that they are. He suggests that the concept of Cthulhu and the Old Ones sleeping under the sea preparatory to hurling themselves on the human race in an orgy of destruction, is essentially Freudian, and can be interpreted as an image of destructive repressions buried in the individual's unconscious. They are quite literally monsters from the Id. It is tempting to assume a connection between the notion of repression and the image of burial, although it should also not be forgotten that the Old Ones came from the stars in the first place; and there is no doubt that Lovecraft would seem at first glance to be a textbook case of every imaginable repression. On the other hand, the essence of repression in Freudian terms is that the desires in question are buried in the sense that their existence is not admitted by the conscious mind of the subject. On this basis, Lovecraft seems to have been remarkably free of repressions. He was genuinely disinterested in sex, and he made no secret at all of his loathing for his fellowmen and most of their activities. He may indeed have been compensating for his own physical deficiencies, but this is a quite different psychological problem. It is perhaps more likely on the whole that the hideous forms and destructive potentialities of the Old Ones really symbolize Lovecraft's ethnic obsessions, as a consequence of which he would be haunted by the vision of an Aryan élite being eventually submerged by a swarm of physically repellent *untermensch* rising from the depths of society.

The basic trouble is of course that, as Wilson himself admits, Lovecraft's literary technique is so hopelessly bad that he never succeeds in imparting any kind of psychological *frisson* to his stories: nobody ever looked seriously for a deeper meaning in anything Lovecraft ever wrote. Nor is Wilson on any surer ground when he tries to exalt Lovecraft as one dedicated to the undermining of materialism, ' declaring passionately that the extraordinary exists '. Lovecraft is, among his other lovable qualities, totally and unreservedly materialistic in his view of life. 'I hate and despise religion', he told Frank Long, 'because it lies about basic, scientifically established facts', with which Lovecraft himself had probably less acquaintance than most even partially educated men of his generation. He reserved the same unmitigated contempt for 'all alleged phenomena of Occultism, Spiritualism and extrasensory perception'. If Lovecraft were indeed an anti-materialist despite himself, one can only hope, for the sake of whatever peace of mind he might ever have known, that he never found it out.

These reflections on Lovecraft appear to have inspired Wilson to try his own hand at the Cthulhu game. He undoubtedly brought to the task immense versatility, a lucid, workmanlike style, a far wider erudition, some acquaintance with human characters, and a genuine flair for dialogue, even if only in three-sentence spurts. This was considerably more equipment than Lovecraft himself ever deployed. Wilson's specific contribution to the Mythos was the *Voynich Manuscript*, first introduced in his story, *The Return of the Lloigor*. The manuscript, we are told, 'was found in an old chest in an Italian castle by a rare book dealer, Wilfred M. Voynich, and brought to the United States in 1912'. It contains references to the *Necronomicon*, which of course draws the narrator's attention to Lovecraft. His researches then lead him to the concept of the drowned continent of Mu in the South Pacific, which he learns was populated by 'invisible ones from the stars', led by Ghatanothoa, the Dark Ones, and known as Lloigor. The Lloigor used men as their slaves as the Old Ones used the Shaggoths. However, the Lloigor became weakened by their existence in a hostile environment, and retreated under the earth and sea, occasionally emerging to take revenge on their former slaves, whenever they can find them. Wilson bolsters the story with accounts of assorted unexplained cataclysms, largely culled from the researches of Charles Fort.

The story is better in almost any sense than any other written on this fundamentally pointless theme, and has of course the added advantage, that by pretending to take Lovecraft seriously, Wilson vastly enhances the verisimilitude of his own tale. In any event, he seems to have been sufficiently encouraged by his success to have followed it with a huge elaboration of the story of the Lloigor in the only, and hopefully the last, novel in the Cthulhu Mythos, *The Philosopher's Stone*. Wilson's intelligence and technique naturally enable him to add dimensions to the Mythos beyond the scope of Lovecraft's decidedly limited talents. We get a fully detailed and rational account of why the Old Ones came to earth, why they in fact created human beings, why and how they took on partially physical form themselves, what happened to them, and why they are so singularly beastly to their former servants. It is all most convincing, because Wilson is capable of writing about fake scientific investigations in an appropriately precise and uncluttered style, which Lovecraft was never able to do. As against that, one must conclude that *The Philosopher's Stone* is far less successful as a novel than *The Return of the Lloigor* is as a short story. In the first place, it is incredibly ill-balanced: the story proper does not begin until two-thirds of the way through the book, the preceding part having been taken up with an all-too-familiar tour of Colin Wilson's mind. We also in fact get a tour of his stomach: for some reason, the reader is informed earlier in the book that the narrator ate lobster thermidor at Wheeler's with a glass of lager for lunch. It has nothing to do with the story, but one has been sufficiently warned already, when Wilson disarmingly remarks that: 'Perhaps it is not entirely relevant to my story, but I cannot resist trying to give a picture of my life at Sneiton in those early years', and proceeds to give a blow-by-blow account of his musical education: 'the complete Contest Between Harmony and Invention of Vivaldi, the complete Well Tempered Clavier, whole operas of Wagner, the last five quartets of Beethoven, symphonies of Bruckner and Mahler, the first fourteen Haydn symphonies'. There is no pretence that any of them have anything to do with the story, any more than have Mr Wilson's views on Shakespeare and Bacon: 'They have something in common. They're both second rate minds.'

One would hesitate to rank Lovecraft even among the second-rate. At the same time, however, there is such a thing as the Lovecraft achievement, which it is perfectly simple to define. He succeeded in influencing a number of other authors, one or two of whom write far better than he could. It is an achievement which is essentially inartistic, in the sense that the man is vastly more significant than his work. Bram Stoker is almost invisible behind the towering figure of Dracula; the vampire ladies flourish where Le Fanu is unknown; Haggard, who was by no means an insignificant personality, lingers in the memory as the reflection of Allan Quatermain; one even thinks of the Devil before thinking of Dennis Wheatley. With Lovecraft, the reverse is the case. There is no Cthulhu Mythos. There is only a Lovecraft Mythos, which will endure for as long as Arkham House finds it profitable to perpetuate it.

6 Orthodox Horrors:
Charles Williams and
William P. Blatty

Until very recent times, it can only have been extra-ordinarily difficult for anybody accepting the principles of orthodox Christianity to cope at all effectively with occult phenomena, let alone write stories about them. In the first place, the Christian laity were specifically debarred from concerning themselves with the occult at all. Even apart from that, occult phenomena other than those involved in the canonization of saints were neces-sarily regarded as works of the Devil, which rendered any kind of objective treatment hardly practicable. Offici-ally appointed exorcists of the Catholic Church were indeed in a different position, but exorcists do not write novels. Nor indeed would it be easy for a practising ortho-dox Christian lay person to make them the subject of a novel, because the kind of diabolical activities they would be concerned with would be of a nature which such a person would be morally inhibited from writing about.

All these problems are strikingly manifested in the works of Charles Williams (1886–1945), the one example of an orthodox lay Christian theologian who also composed a number of substantial works of fiction dealing essentially with occult themes. His efforts were in fact substantially unsuccessful, for reasons which will be examined later.

D

The fact that his novels are still being republished can thus only be regarded as a tribute to his undoubted literary and intellectual gifts, rather than to the attractions of the stories themselves. There is at least no doubt as to the qualities of the former. Williams was incomparably the most academically distinguished of all the writers of occult fiction. He was poet, historian, theologian, critic, lecturer in the City Library Institute and editor at the Oxford University Press. He also possessed of necessity the advantage that he actually believed in the supernatural, as Haggard certainly did, as Dennis Wheatley and Le Fanu apparently did, as Stoker may have done and as Lovecraft emphatically did not. Moreover, his enormous knowledge of and sympathy with both Christian and Islamic theology enabled him to conceive plots of a philosophical complexity and logical coherence that other writers of occult fiction were simply not intellectually equipped to handle. For example, his first novel, *Shadows of Ecstasy*, deals with the theme of employing the primitive witchcraft of Africa to overthrow European civilization. *War in Heaven* combined the Arthurian myth of the quest for the Holy Grail with Wheatley-type satanism. *Many Dimensions* uses Islamic theology as well as the Christian interpretation of natural law as backgrounds to a story superficially about travel through space and time. *Descent Into Hell* employs the Christian ideas of martyrdom and purgatory, reinforced with a certain amount of reincarnation, a doppelganger and a succubus. The principal characters of *All Hallows' Eve* are in fact already dead when the story opens, inhabiting a Christian limbo. *The Place of the Lion* combines the beatific vision of the Christian mystics with the Platonic concept of the materialization of the Forms. There is a richness and variety of occult fauna and flora here which really cannot be approached anywhere else in fiction.

The practical problem is to define why it all fails to

work. Williams' deficiencies are admittedly neither literary nor personal. He was an immensely cultured, humane
and even humorous man, and a profound literary artist.
He was also quite simply totally unsuited to the craft of
fiction. His failings in this area comprised a total inability
to write idiomatic or even credible dialogue; a total lack
of interest in the depicting and development of character;
and a complete failure to appreciate the amount of
esoteric philosophy that even an unusually thoughtful
reader of occult fiction is likely to be in a mood to
appreciate. This is not to say that Williams is a difficult
writer to read, nor that there is no place for philosophy
in fiction. Meredith is for example far more difficult, and
probably more philosophical. But one is prepared to
grapple with Meredith's tortured syntax for the sake of
discovering what happens to his incredibly vital characters, and for the enjoyment of his brilliant dialogue. It is
precisely Williams' characters and dialogue that leave one
utterly undisposed to endure his philosophy.

Ironically, although Williams' plots became intrinsically more interesting with each succeeding novel, his
deficiencies as a novelist became more glaring. *War in
Heaven*, for example, has a simple and even familiar
story, once one appreciates that the Grail is spelt Graal
throughout; there is a certain amount of action, including
something very close to a fight; the dialogue is not good
but is less irritatingly unidiomatic than in his later and
more profound novels; and there is the nearest approach
to an erotic sequence in all of Williams' writings, when
Barbara Rackstraw, the alleged heroine of the story, is
possessed of demonic forces, and 'still moving in that
wild dance, tore her light frock and underwear from the
breast downwards. It hung, ripped and rent, from the
girdle that caught it together; then it fell lower, and she
shook her legs free without checking the movement of the
dance.' The scene is the more remarkable in that Williams

never again refers to the clothes worn by his characters, let alone to the possibility of their ever taking them off. But it is hardly enough to sustain interest, given the tremendous technical deficiencies of Williams' characterization. One is for a start not given even the slightest impression of the physical appearance of the *dramatis personae*. Nor is one given much impression of what goes on inside their minds. They are one-dimensional beyond the limits of monomania. There is an archdeacon whose mind runs endlessly on tricky points of theology; a duke of the North Ridings who thinks only of the ancestral glories of his House; Barbara Rackstraw, who does not think at all; and Barbara's husband, whose thoughts are only of the possibility of her being unfaithful to him, and what a hell of a life it is generally.

The novel also introduces Williams' long-term villain, Sir Giles Tumulty. The names are obviously intended to evoke images of Gilles de Raiz and tumult equals disorder equals the Lord of Misrule. As resident devil-figure, he is necessarily central to the development of the novels in which he appears. His effect is however nullified by the fact that Williams has him exhibit his wickedness chiefly through the medium of what may quite seriously be the worst dialogue ever written. 'The thing that'll keep you safe is that no one with more brains than a gutter-bred snipe like that Archdeacon would think your collection of middle-class platitudes worth adding to', he remarks to one of his allies. 'I'll see that lurching sewer-rat in Hinnom before I spend good money on him' is also rather unconvincing. The trouble is indeed that all Williams' characters are so unconvincing that they are virtually invisible, so that the reader has immense difficulty in trying to remember who they are, let alone develop any interest in what might happen to them. It is in fact genuinely difficult to understand what is supposed to be happening: where there are no characters, there is no motivation, and without motivation action becomes incomprehensible. To make matters worse, Williams is prone to interlard the narrative on any page with passages like the following: 'The cause of all action there disposed itself according to that Will which was its nature, and, so disposing itself, moved him easily as a part of its own accommodation to the changing wills of men, so that at any time and at all times its own perfection was maintained, now known in endurance, now in beauty, now in wisdom.' The sentence is beautifully constructed, from an architectural point of view. However, it is not even lucid, and the presence of such material in a novel, even it were more clearly expressed, could only act as the most effective deterrent to the reader.

The merits and demerits of *War in Heaven* are both exhibited in intensified form in the two later major novels, *The Place of the Lion* and *Many Dimensions*. Both display a brilliance of imaginative conception far more intriguing than the rather tawdry satanism of *War in Heaven*. *The Place of the Lion* for example begins with the tremendous image of a gigantic and clearly preternatural lion standing over the body of a man on the Hertfordshire road. Other monstrous archetypes make their appearance later. The rationale is nothing less than a variation on Plato's theory of the Forms:

this world is created, and all men and women are created, by the entrance of certain great principles into aboriginal matter. We call them by cold names; wisdom and courage and beauty and strength and so on, but actually they are very great and mighty Powers.... And when That which is behind them intends to put a new soul into matter it disposes them as it will, and by a peculiar mingling of them a child is born. . . . In the animals they are less mingled, for there each is shown to us in his own becoming shape; those Powers are the archetypes of the beasts, and very much more.... Generally, matter is the separation between all these animals which we know and the powers beyond. But if one of those animals should be brought within the terrific influence of one particular idea ... the matter of the beast might be changed into the image of the idea, and this world, following that one, might all be drawn into that other world.

The implications are genuinely fascinating, although, given a choice, one might well prefer to take one's Plato straight, rather than blurred by the intrusions of an alien theology. What Williams conceives it all to mean in practice is indicated by the most effective scene of the transmutation of the malevolent Miss Wilmot into the archetypal snake.

But the problem once again is in the characterization, which is even more aggressively bad than in *War in Heaven*. The heroine, who bears the disconcerting name of Damaris Tighe, is a pedantic young Ph.D. candidate who is preparing a dissertation on the topic of the correct evaluation of the concentric cultural circles of Hellenic and pre-mediaeval cosmology. This indeed might seem to be a matter of specialized and decidedly limited interest. It is however basic to the development of the plot, because the action flows from her failure to appreciate the actual significance of the concepts with which the neo-Platonic philosophers were dealing. One might remark that it is at least a new idea for a thriller. Her errors are pointed out to her by her selfless and virtually bodiless lover Anthony, in speeches like: 'You are the Sherbet of Allah, and the gold cup he drinks it out of.... You are the Night of Repose and the Day of Illumination. You are, incidentally, a night with a good deal of rain and a day with a nasty cold wind ... *O quanta qualia*.... Those something sabbaths the blessed ones see.' She counters with the devastating retort: 'Don't you even know what a philosophic universal is?' What is at least clear by this time is the nature of the public Williams is writing for: his books are directed at Oxbridge-educated Anglican neo-Platonists about to enter enclosed religious orders.

Even such a select group might possibly be disturbed by passages of undergraduate fooling which can only be described as sheer self-indulgence on Williams' part, since they add nothing to the development of the novel itself. Anthony, for example,

> unthinkingly ... put out his hand to the cigarette box which Quentin had given him one Christmas; given both of them, as he had himself pointed out, in remarking on the superior nature of his own present, which had been a neat kind of pocket-book and therefore an entirely personal gift. But Quentin had maintained that the cigarette box, as being of greater good to a greater number, had been nearer to the ideal perfection of giving. 'For,' he had argued, 'to give to you a means by which you can give to others, is better than to give a merely private thing.'
>
> 'But,' Anthony had persisted, 'in so far as you are one of those others – and likely to be the most persistent – you give to yourself and therefore altogether deprive the act of the principle of giving.'

All very true, no doubt; but one would need to possess quite unusual intellectual and spiritual qualities to be able to endure many passages like that in a work of occult fiction.

The Place of the Lion is thus both better and worse than *War In Heaven*. The underlying concept is more original and arresting, the action more vivid, the style more magnificent, the characterization more incompetent and incredible, the dialogue more unidiomatic and infuriating, and the intellectual atmosphere more stupefying. Williams shows his best qualities as a writer in those works where he shows his worst qualities as a novelist.

He attains both his zenith and his nadir in *Many Dimensions*. The basic idea is again marvellous. It involves, to put it simply, the discovery of the Stone of Solomon, which contains the universe within itself, and can accordingly grant its possessor the power to move at will through time and space. It comes into the hands of Sir Giles Tumulty, who is seized by the superbly prosaic notion of founding a transport company, using the Stone as its motive power, and thus becoming the richest man in the world. He is encouraged, if hardly aided, by his inane but rapacious stockbroker nephew, Reginald Montague, who is Williams' closest approach to a credible character. It is incidentally interesting to reflect that the most life-like character in Williams' stories should be the one with whom on all counts Williams himself must have felt the least affinity. At all events, their attempts to exploit the Stone in the interests of capitalist enterprise involve them in admirably satirized confrontations with the trade unions, who are alarmed at the prospect of their comrades in the public transport systems being made redundant, as well as in some practical problems, also finely conceived. Tumulty for example experiments with the Stone to save the life of a criminal awaiting execution by hanging. He survives, all right, but only as a consciousness without voice or movement, having suffered all the other physical side-effects of having had his neck broken. The actual occult moments themselves are handled possibly even better than in *The Place of the Lion*, the scene of Tumulty's own descent into hell being undoubtedly the most vivid and intellectually satisfying of all descriptions of that particular experience:

> The light leaped out at him, and suddenly Giles Tumulty began to scream. For at once the light and

with it the pain passed through him, dividing nerve from nerve, sinew from sinew, bone from bone. Everywhere the sharp torment caught him, and still, struggling and twisting, he was dragged down the curving spirals nearer to the illumination into which he was already plunged.... He was conscious also of a myriad other Giles Tumultys, of childhood and boyhood and youth and age, all that he had ever been, and all of them were screaming as that relentless and dividing light plunged into them and held them. He was doing, it seemed, innumerable things at once, all the things that he had ever done, and yet the whole time he was not doing, he was slipping, slipping down.... When they found him, but a few moments after that raucous scream had terrified the household, he was lying on the floor amid the shattered furniture twisted in every limb, and pierced and burnt all over as if by innumerable needle-points of fire.

Once again the weaknesses lie in the characterization. Giles' main antagonist is his relative, Lord Arglay, Chief Justice of England, who is engaged on a book entitled *The Survey of Organic Law*, which expresses a mystical view of the nature of English law which few English lawyers would be likely to share. He is all-wise and all-pompous. His chief ally proves to be his secretary, Chloe Burnett, who we are told has experienced a 'throbbing past' with her squalid boyfriend Frank Lindsay. She indeed seems to have all but gone the whole way: 'their hands and their mouths, their voices and their glances, were familiar. All but the sovereign union had been theirs.' Chloe Burnett has however clearly found sex unrewarding: 'Was there any devotion beyond the sudden overwhelming madness of sex? And in that hot airless tunnel of emotion what pleasure was there and what joy? Laughter died there, and lucidity, and the clear intelligence she loved, and there was nothing of the peace for which she hungered.' At the very least, this is hardly an adequate view of human relations. Williams is in fact at his unhappiest and most stilted when discussing human relations in any form, which only reinforces the argument that he was temperamentally unsuited to writing fiction in the first place. There is certainly no overwhelming madness in Chloe's relationship with the chief justice, who invariably refers to her and thinks of her as a 'child'. On the single occasion when she makes a pass at him he concludes instantly and quite correctly that she must be possessed by the Devil, or at least by Giles Tumulty. The scene is significant in another way: just as Bram Stoker's women are interesting only when they are turning into vampires, Williams' are interesting only when possessed by evil forces. This does not necessarily symbolize any great truth about human life. It is not true that good is intrinsically less interesting than evil. It just takes more talent to write about it.

Even on a philosophical level, Williams is not wholly satisfactory. The whole rationale of *The Place of the Lion* for example is the hero's successful struggle to prevent the material universe from being absorbed into the forms which are invading it. But this would logically be the best thing that could possibly happen to the material universe, if it is in fact only an imperfect materialization of the forms, a reflection of true reality which is also true beauty. It would be like trying to hold off the Second Coming. The dilemma in *Many Dimensions* is even more profound. Williams' world-view is totally and fundamentally Anglican. But the occult aspects of the story are drawn from Islamic theology. Tumulty outrages Christian values, but he descends into a Moslem hell, observed by Moslem saints and angels. Similarly, when Chloe achieves her sovereign union with the Stone one is left to assume that she is consequently transported to either a Moslem paradise or a Buddhist nirvana. Under the circumstances, her destination could scarcely be a Christian heaven.

The work of William P. Blatty constitutes in every possible way a total contrast to that of Charles Williams. It is in the first place vastly more popular: Williams' public is of necessity limited to those with the necessary qualities of intellect, temperament and endurance; Blatty's fifth and most famous novel, ⌈The Exorcist, was on the other hand the most successful bestseller in the United States in the year of its publication,⌉ and the film version became the third greatest box-office success in cinema history. It also achieved legal significance, in being cited by defence counsel in a number of criminal cases on behalf of clients pleading that they had become possessed while watching the film, and were therefore not responsible for any rapes, murders or assaults they might have committed afterwards.

It may be said that Blatty triumphs totally over all the theological inhibitions which rendered Williams' works unsuccessful as novels. The fact that his characters are mainly members of the Roman Catholic priesthood does not in the slightest impede the introduction of sex and violence into the story. There are admittedly no explicit erotic relationships of any kind between people, apart from a hint of latent homosexuality on the part of the exorcist himself. However, Blatty positively succeeds in introducing new dimensions of sex and violence when he depicts a pre-adolescent girl masturbating with a crucifix. There are also positive litanies of all the more familiar slang words for the sexual act and the associated organs. The use of obscenities in the dialogue is genuinely start-ling, not only because of what is said, but even more because of who is saying it. The possessed girl's mother confesses to herself that ' old mother's ass is draggin'' when she goes to her daughter's room to investigate disturbing noises at night. Priests say ' shit ' on every possible occasion, and refer to one another as 'assholes'. Blatty's dialogue could certainly never be termed unidiomatic: it is in fact vulgar beyond credibility. We are worlds away from Charles Williams' Oxbridge Anglicans at play.

The impact of the dialogue in Blatty's story is reinforced by a prose style that uses images like a baseball bat. An Arab roustabout on the take in Iraq 'stood waiting like an ancient debt'; a beer truck lumbers by 'with a clink of quivering warm, wet promises', which would certainly tend to evoke thoughts of something other than a drink of beer, which is more welcome cool than warm, in any case; a priest tormented by problems of faith takes the Host and 'swallowed the papery taste of despair', or on another occasion 'swallowed the Host like lost illusion'. The imagery in this and other instances is not merely obtrusive, it is also inappropriate: there is no way in which one can even envisage swallowing a lost illusion.

As against this, Blatty is an extremely skilful master of complex narrative. The mechanics of *The Exorcist* are admittedly nowhere near as elaborate or varied as those of *Dracula*. It is nonetheless one of the few novels which give the reader the added pleasure of watching a taut and coherent pattern of cause and effect reveal itself. The past gives forewarnings of the present; the present becomes intelligible only with reference back to the past; and the added dimension of the occult gives resonance and significance to physical events. These indeed have sufficient impact of their own. On the most basic level, *The Exorcist* would have to be the most obscene and revolting book ever written: the possessed girl masturbates, urinates, defaecates, vomits and spits throughout most of the story, and Blatty in no way shrinks from the task of describing faithfully what is going on. It might also seem to be the most blasphemous: Blatty may not have mentioned every physically possible act of disrespect that can be done with a crucifix or a holy statue, but he must surely have mentioned every one that is actually worth doing.

Blasphemy is however by no means Blatty's intention. It is also in no way the effect of the book. The theme of the book is religious in the strictest possible sense: its message is that even those who cannot believe in God can recover a trust in personal immortality by becoming aware of the existence of the Devil. It is in fact the message of *The Brothers Karamazov*. Blatty also takes the trouble to get his facts and his ideas right: the author's note appended to the English edition of the book claims that Blatty had read every book published in English on the subject of possession, so he was in a position to tell us more about it than we ever wanted to know. More importantly, his theology is absolutely consistent, which one may suggest is more than Williams' is: we are in the domain of the Roman Catholic Church, in both the physical and spiritual universes, without any intrusions from Islam, Buddhism or other occult systems.

The Exorcist in other words is fundamentally successful as a novel. Blatty has not been a Hollywood script-writer for nothing: he can handle dialogue, describe character adequately, discover credible motivations, and generally move the story along. He can also construct a remarkably tidy and intrinsically interesting plot. Nor does one put down *The Exorcist* feeling swamped by images of guilt and repression as with Stoker and Le Fanu, or with the sense of having been treated to an exercise in pornography as with Wheatley. The main criticism of *The Exorcist* is indeed that it is hard to see how this can be other than a once-for-all attempt. Unlike Haggard, who could follow the adventures of his great archetypes literally endlessly through different incarnations and different levels of existence, Blatty would really seem to have fired every shot in that particular locker: his pet demon, Puzazu, may indeed return to strike again, but there is really nothing new for him to do. One would not really welcome a repeat of *The Exorcist*. Blatty has already said it all.[1]

This is all the more pertinent because *The Exorcist* has been followed by a non-fictional study of possession written by ex-Jesuit Father Malachi Martin, *Hostage of the Devil*, which recounts his own experiences as an exorcist, providing fully documented reports on the possession and exorcism of five living Americans. Father Martin is emphatic about the occult nature of possession, about the existence of the Devil as 'a bodiless spirit created by God that is the pole of this universe', and on the frequent and even commonplace nature of the phenomena he describes with, according to his reviewers 'a sexual explicitness ... which makes William Peter Blatty's *The Exorcist* as sinister as the Tooth Fairy'. This can only be over-stating the case, but Father Martin would nonetheless seem to have pre-empted the market: nobody would really want to read dirty novels about exorcism, when there are even dirtier documentary studies available.

7 The Devil and Dennis Wheatley

There are many reasons why Dennis Wheatley seriously deserves to be regarded as one of the most remarkable literary phenomena of our time. He is to begin with the most financially successful writer on the occult in the English language. Bram Stoker's *Dracula* has indeed out-sold any single one of Dennis Wheatley's books, but Stoker's other books would scarcely have sold at all but for *Dracula*, while at least four of Wheatley's tales of the supernatural have been regularly reprinted in hard covers over the past forty years. The sheer magnitude of his publishing success commands respect in its own right: in a literary career which has continued uninterrupted since 1932, Wheatley has sold more than thirty million copies of his books in twenty-seven languages. Success has been a way of life for Dennis Wheatley: the family wine business in which he began his career was patronized by three kings and twenty-one princes, as well as by un-counted millionaires; he has written with success on Charles II, the Russian Revolution and the Second World War, as well as on the occult; and at the age of eighty he has just published his first volume of memoirs, with the promise of at least four more volumes to follow.[1]

All this might not make Dennis Wheatley a great novel-ist, but it undoubtedly makes him a literary phenomenon deserving close examination. This is all the more the case because his work contains a number of incongruities which can only be termed baffling. He is for example a totally serious, self-conscious student of the occult, who has written a non-fictional study on the subject, *The Devil and All His Works*, and has used his novels as vehicles for the expression of the most coherently developed theory of the occult put forward by any English novelist, apart from J. B. Priestley. On the other hand, his personal attitude to the occult hardly seems to chime with his intellectual beliefs. He disclaims any actual experience of that area of human existence, assuring his readers in the prefatory note to his most famous novel of the occult, *The Devil Rides Out* that he personally had 'never assisted at, or participated in, any ceremony connected with Magic – Black or White'. In other words, he had got it all from books, as well as from 'conversation with certain persons, sought out for that purpose, who are actual practitioners of the art'. Forty years later, he warned the readers of *The Devil and All His Works* that 'by participating in Satanic Rites, however sham, one can make oneself a focus for Evil'. The advice is no doubt good, but it comes a trifle oddly from the person who has undoubtedly made more financially out of the general business of satanic rites than any actual practitioner.

There are however far stranger aspects to Dennis Wheatley. His novels of the occult are not merely vehicles for a profound and coherent view of the forces operating outside the limits of the physical universe. They are also and to an almost equal extent vehicles for a political world-view somewhat to the right of Charles II. On every indication, Wheatley is monarchist, chauvinist, racist and individualist, or at least assumes that his readers would like to think he is. For example, in *Strange Conflict*, undoubtedly the queerest and probably the worst of his

stories of the occult, we are informed that 'these coloured
bums have no powers of organization at all', and that by
contrast 'as long as Britain stands the Powers of Darkness
cannot prevail. On Earth the Anglo-Saxon race is the last
Guardian of the Light, and I have an unshakeable conviction that, come what may, ours is and will prove the
bulwark of the world.'

In *The Haunting of Toby Jugg*, Wheatley's best occult
story, and technically one of the best of all stories of the
genre, we are abruptly told that the election of foreigners
to the House of Commons is a 'monstrous perversion in
the representation of the British people', and that
'socialist economics have chained the masses and are
relentlessly pressing them into a pattern so that in another
generation they will be no more than human robots'. In
Star of Ill-Omen, which combines anti-communism, sex
and flying saucers, the hero exclaims: 'There isn't much
real freedom anywhere today; but what there is, I,
personally, would go to any lengths to preserve.' One
really cannot seriously doubt that in these and similar
statements the author is speaking in his own voice. In the
first place, they are completely extraneous to the stories
themselves, and can hardly be introduced to widen their
appeal: sex and violence really do not need reactionary
politics to enhance their attractiveness. Moreover,
Wheatley has not hesitated to express his political views at
a time when they might well have rendered him liable
to the attentions of the censor: in *Come Into My Parlour*,
written at the most critical period of the Second World
War, he makes his hero, Gregory Sallust, speak as if the
Allied cause were scarcely worth fighting for, and as if
the most dangerous enemy of the British people were their
own Government: 'The bureaucrats have at last got us
where they've wanted us for years. This war is being used
as an excuse to strangle all free enterprise, and to prevent
any Englishman's home ever being his castle any more....

We'll all be dreary little people living in dreary little houses and forced to work eight hours a day in some ghastly factory making luxury goods for export to our richer neighbours.'

One can hardly doubt Wheatley's sincerity, any more than one can deny him a certain prophetic vision. It might even seem reasonable to suppose that a man haunted by so despairing a picture of the future of the physical universe might well turn his attention to the form of an occult universe, which could only hold more promise for mankind, as it could not possibly hold less. This does seem in fact to be the case: Wheatley's view of the physical universe is explicitly Manichean, or more accurately Platonic, in that he sees it as essentially a place to which the soul is exiled from its true home. Such a concept of course essentially corresponds in practice to Rider Haggard's conviction that this world is one of the hells. This however would be the only respect in which the names of Wheatley and Haggard could be linked. The most striking and disturbing anomaly of Wheatley's work is precisely the respect in which he differs most radically from Haggard. This simply is in his attitude to sex.

Haggard, as has been seen, is one of the most erotic and least titillating of writers. His whole body of work can be regarded as a statement of the belief that love can be sought meaningfully only beyond the grave, as symbolized in the archetypal if distinctly confusing figure of Ayesha. By contrast, Dennis Wheatley's approach is wholly unerotic, and titillating above all else. There is literally no symbolism in his occult stories, no images of unadmitted or concealed desires, no goddess-figures whose love reaches across repeated incarnations or down from an astral plane of being. One gets instead the unabashed presentation of woman as a sexual object, to be exhibited, enjoyed, raped, tortured and on occasion murdered. Indeed, the paraphernalia of the occult itself is introduced not for any

symbolic purpose, but simply to provide opportunities for
the exposure and abuse of the heroine.[2] Wheatley may
well be the most aggressive and consistent male chauvinist
in fiction: indeed he could be described as a trail-blazer
in this regard. *Come Into My Parlour* contains the first
fictional description of a woman undergoing torture by
being impaled with electrodes. It also contains an episode
in which Gregory Sallust, after making love to a voluptuous and meticulously-described German woman, shoots
her, first in the back and then in the head, because 'the
lower part of her body *was* her life to Helga, and she
wouldn't be much use to anyone or herself without the
use of it. . . . He felt no compunction at all about the act.
It was the merciful thing to do.' In *V for Vengeance*
Sallust persuades another German girl to remove her
stockings by threatening to punch her nose through the
back of her head if she refuses. *The Shadow of Tyburn
Tree* contains the first description in ostensibly respectable
English fiction of a woman being sexually flagellated,
with of all instruments, an umbrella. In this episode, the
hero, a patriotic young Englishman named Roger Brook,
finds a Russian princess naked, punches her in the belly,
spanks her senseless and prepares to rape her, in the
interests of British foreign policy. The flagellation theme
is expanded in *Curtain of Fear*, which also contains
Wheatley's most fervent apostrophes to God, the Queen
and England, and was dedicated to the Bishop of London.
Wheatley's treatment of sex in his fiction is however not
confined to the description of rape and torture. He is also
unexcelled as an observer of stocking-tops.[3]

One might be inclined to feel that a man who consistently writes at this kind of level could not write seriously
about anything. But nothing is simple about Dennis
Wheatley. It is for example certainly intriguing to note
that Gregory Sallust himself is described as having a
satanic appearance, and unquestionably possesses the

qualities of a demon rather than of a human being. But there is no suggestion at all that Sallust is in fact supposed to be regarded as being demonic in any occult sense. He is on the contrary presented as being invariably on the side of the angels, and in many ways not unlike Wheatley himself, who was also 'of good middle-class stock.... He was an imaginative and therefore troublesome boy and after only two and a half terms was expelled for innumerable breaches of discipline from his public school, Dulwich College.' Sallust's satanic appearance is most likely inspired by Dashiell Hammett's Sam Spade, who is described by his creator as 'looking like a blonde Satan', and who made his fictional debut in 1929, five years before Mr Wheatley published the first volume in the Sallust saga, *Black August*.

Sallust's sadism goes beyond the murder and abuse of women. In *Come Into My Parlour*, he uses a silk handkerchief for a knuckleduster, so that 'the silk, catching under heavy pressure on the skin, ripped it open as though it had been slashed with a knife and blood poured from the gaping wound. It was a trick that Gregory had learnt, long ago in Paris, from an Apache'. Wheatley however presents him as a thoroughly admirable personality. Lady Veronica Wensleadale, in *Black August* is referring to Sallust when she confesses that she has 'always been attracted to the type of blackguard who has brains and guts providing they have a sense of humour and the decencies'. Apart from the fact that a blackguard is by definition bereft of decency, there is of course never any indication that Sallust in particular possesses either of those qualifications. One can only assume however that Wheatley, like his heroine, was quite unaware of this.

There is no reason to imagine that Dennis Wheatley has ever been aware of the existence of any incongruity in the situation of a novelist of the occult, whose continuing theme is the struggle between the forces of good and evil, having a demon-figure for his favourite hero. A man who could dedicate to the Bishop of London a book which opened new horizons in sex and sadism is not likely to be too sensitive to incongruities or even lapses of taste. Self-criticism of any kind is the quality one least associates with Dennis Wheatley. Once again, however, it is impossible to give an unqualified judgement. The combination of sex, sadism and the occult would doubtless have guaranteed massive popular success for Wheatley even if he had been as bad a writer as Bram Stoker or as uneven a one as Rider Haggard. His success has no doubt been made all the greater because he is one of the most fluent writers of his time. His sentences are almost unfailingly pleasant to the ear, carefully punctuated, grammatically constructed and organized with a real sense of rhetorical effect. As a master of narrative, he is in the same category if not on the same level as Thackeray or George M. Trevelyan. The trouble is that his sentences are excellent until one starts looking at the words. Wheatley can seriously claim to be the greatest living master of the cliché. One can find on almost every page whole passages that might have been assembled by a computer, programmed to regurgitate nothing but certified banalities, as for example in this alleged love scene from *Star of Ill-Omen*: 'Flushed and trembling, she had consented. Once inside, their passion mounted to fever heat.... During hours that sped all too swiftly, they gave free rein to the lovely madness that had seized upon them both, and, quite oblivious of past or future, revelled in the highest delights that youth can give.'

With this bewildering array of incompatible qualities, Wheatley could only be a most unusual novelist of the occult. He has no doubt many of the negative qualifications, such as a style capable at its worst of such banalities as to become almost meaningless, a total lack of concern for human personalities or human situations and an abiding concern with the less conventional aspects of sex. On the other hand, he is equally unconcerned to explore these aspects through the medium of symbolism, he seems himself to be acquainted with no passions at all save those associated with politics, and he has denied having any direct experience of or affinities for the occult at all. What he has brought to the genre is a very substantial store of historical knowledge, an inexhaustible energy in narrative, and a profound and even noble philosophy which seems to be absolutely unrelated to every other aspect of his life and work.

Dennis Wheatley's most famous novel of the occult is probably his first, *The Devil Rides Out*, published in 1934. It is certainly not his best: the plot can only be described as an undirected blur of events quite incapable of being summarized, and the characters exist only as names, with the possible exception of the Duc de Richelieu, who lingers vaguely in the memory only because he is made the vehicle for some of Wheatley's views on the good life. We are told that the Duc 'did not subscribe to the canon which has branded ostentation as vulgarity in the last few generations'. To prove the point, he consumes 'a long Hoyo de Monterrey and wonderful old brandy in a bowl-shaped glass across a low jade bowl with trailing sprays of orchids', while wearing a 'claret-coloured vicuna smoking suit with silk lapels and braided fastenings'. The actual physical description leaves something to be desired, but the atmosphere of unabashed luxury might have made agreeable reading in 1934: luxury might well have been more exciting than sex to the imagination in the darkest years of the depression. In any case, the conventions of the time made it impossible for Wheatley to be as explicitly titillating as he could be ten years later. His descriptions of the more potentially pornographic aspects of occult ritual are indeed positively inhibited.

The term *osculam-infame* is left unexplained and untranslated; the nine openings of the body which are to be sealed against invasion of evil spirits are hastily summarized as 'eyes, nostrils, lips, etc'; at a high point of the Black Mass 'a great silver chalice was being passed from hand to hand, and very soon he realized the purpose to which it was being put', although the reader is left to guess: and when de Richelieu prepares the heroine's body for some advanced occult experiences, the rest of the company 'gazed obediently at the book-lined walls while he did certain curious things', which are similarly left to the reader's imagination.

An occult novel lacking a well-constructed plot or memorable characters and devoid alike of erotic symbolism or explicit sexuality would hardly seem predestined for success. In fact, the sales of *The Devil Rides Out* have been exceeded only by those of *Dracula* in this area of fiction. The reasons are twofold. In the first place, it is simply true that Dennis Wheatley is unmatched as an inventor of incident: there is literally always something happening in the story, and the rush of events is the more compelling in that it is never interrupted for even the most cursory examination of character or motivation. Nobody ever got on with the story like Dennis Wheatley. Even more important, the novel tells one more about the occult than any other written at that time. *The Devil Rides Out* is totally successful as a painless introduction to the occult sciences: there are allusions to the Sepher Ha Zoher, the Sepher Jetyirah and the Midraschim; to the six stages of Probatione, Neophye, Zelator, Practicus, Philosophus and Dominus Liminis before one attains to Adeptus Inferior; and to the last two lines of the dread Sassuma ritual, which are never to be uttered except when the soul is in peril of destruction, and which Wheatley understandably does not utter, even in print. There is no cheaper or less intellectually demanding way in which to acquire a superficial familiarity with occult terms than to read *The Devil Rides Out*.

One can never be sure about anything with Dennis Wheatley; but it is unlikely that *The Devil Rides Out* should be dismissed simply as a pretentious confidence-trick. There are features which imply very convincingly that he is taking his subject with real seriousness. There is for example a specific rejection of orthodox Christian theology, which a person of Wheatley's background is not likely to associate himself with lightly: 'there is a power existing outside us which is not peculiar to any religion... There is no such person as the Devil, but there are vast numbers of Earthbound spirits, Elementals and Evil Intelligences of the Outer Circle floating in our midst.' Even more serious is an unreserved endorsement of Manicheism, which Wheatley goes so far as to say is even today believed by many thinking people all over the world to hold the 'core of the only true religion'. One may perhaps believe in the Sassuma ritual or disbelieve in the Devil without any very strong emotions on the subject; but nobody ever embraced Manicheism with a light heart. Nor indeed could one conceive a less likely Manichee than Dennis Wheatley.

He is nonetheless very clearly a serious one. Any suspicion that Manicheism might have simply formed part of the general miscellany of occult data assembled for *The Devil Rides Out* is effectively dissipated by its reappearance seven years later in *Strange Conflict*. This is undoubtedly Wheatley's silliest and worst story. Its basic theme concerns the efforts of British Intelligence to cope with the discovery that German spies have found ways to enter the astral plane and participate in the dreams of their opponents. The action wanders aimlessly over Western Europe and the West Indies. However, in the middle of what can only be termed nonsense one comes across a passage like this:

In its highest sense Light symbolizes the growth of the spirit towards that perfection in which it becomes Light itself. But the road to perfection is long and arduous, too much to hope for in one short human life; hence the widespread belief in reincarnation.... This doctrine is so old that no man can trace its origin, yet it is the inner core of Truth common to all religions at their inception.

It is followed by this salute to Manicheism:

Appolonius of Tyana learned it in the East. The so-called heretics whom we know as the Albigenses preached it in the twelfth century throughout southern France until they were exterminated. Christian Rosenkreutz had it in the Middle Ages; it was the innermost secret of the Order of the Templars, who were suppressed because of it by the Church of Rome; the alchemists too searched for and practised it.

It is impossible not to believe that Dennis Wheatley is genuinely concerned about Manicheism. It is equally difficult to understand how a person seriously possessed of such a philosophy could without any evidence of psychological strain accept the other systems of values which one associates with Wheatley, and which he expounds with equal enthusiasm elsewhere in his novels.

Dennis Wheatley's literary talents and occult perceptions reached their highest expression in *The Haunting of Toby Jugg*, which is in every way his best story, and is certainly comparable with *Dracula*, in terms of its success both as an exercise in literary technique and as a study in the occult. Wheatley certainly writes far better than Stoker; his sense of characterization is at least no worse; and on this occasion he actually employs a simple and tightly controlled plot. It is in fact probably true that the success of the book is due more than anything else to the

fact that the hero is crippled, and therefore physically incapable of setting off on the endless peregrinations which
make Wheatley's other stories simply incoherent yarns.
The plot centres around the plight of the hero, Albert
Abel Jugg, who is temporarily rendered immobile by a
war wound, and is forced in consequence to lie helpless
in his bedroom while a manifestation of evil outside his
window becomes every night more tangible and more
recognizable. It is the classical nightmare situation, in fact.
Wheatley adds a further turn of the screw with the
element of betrayal: Jugg is at the mercy of his aunt and
his lover, who are supposed to be assisting his recovery,
but are in fact plotting to have him driven insane so that
the family fortune can fall into their hands, to be used in
the service of satanism. The dénouement is both convincing in terms of the story, and dramatically satisfying in its
use of coincidence. *The Haunting of Toby Jugg* admittedly lacks the tremendous technical skill of *Dracula*, as it
lacks totally anything of its symbolic power, but its superb
orchestration of terror and rigorously structured plot
entitle it to be regarded as a classic story of the occult in
its own right.

The Haunting of Toby Jugg is of course not impeccable. Along with merits which Wheatley never showed
in any other novel, it has all the blemishes which he has
shown in every other novel. It contains for example his
longest tirades against creeping socialism and the infiltra-
tion of foreigners into British institutions, which can only
be regarded here as totally irrelevant distractions. It also
reflects his characteristic attitude towards women. Toby
Jugg, who really has nothing funny about him apart from
his name, has spent his youth at an independent school
whose curriculum is in effect that of a brothel. His only
hope of rescue, literally in this world and the next, is his
nurse, Sally Cardew, whom he describes as 'a Junoesque
wench, and it would take a man of my size to pick her up

and spank her, but she has one hell of a good figure'.
Sally falls into the hands of the satanists towards the end
of the story and is duly stripped naked, preparatory to
being raped, 'spreadeagled upon a bed of nettles'. The
fact that she is the only one of Wheatley's heroines, who,
being placed in a position to be raped, actually escapes
that fate, is probably quite unimportant. What is important is that Sally, described in the book as 'a hefty wench
with a freckled face, a nice, healthy English hoyden, not
over-burdened with brains', delivers a speech on the
general topic of reincarnation, which is of course completely out of character, but which may stand as
Wheatley's most comprehensive confession of faith:

> It is the only creed which provides a logical explana-
> tion to any and every human experience ... when we
> have learnt all there is to learn here we join the great
> ones who have preceded us.... Such thoughts have been
> instilled into them by generations of ignorant priests
> who have blindly followed the teachings of churches
> that long ago became decadent and lost the light.
> Death is really only a release from trial and hardship
> ... between our lives here, while our spirits are no longer
> imprisoned in a dull and heavy body, we are infinitely
> more fully our real selves, and have a far greater
> capacity for understanding ... it follows that a greater
> number of the friends we have made in our many lives
> are always away from the earth than on it, so we have
> the joy of being with them again. In what we call life,
> we are really only half-alive, but constantly beset by
> troubles, sometimes by ill-health and often lonely;
> whereas what we call death is really living to the full,
> without material worries or physical handicaps, and
> being happy in the company of those we love.

It is a lucid and moving exposition of a noble theory
which would not be out of place in a study of Plato and

Swedenborg: nor is it too incongruous in *The Haunting of Toby Jugg*. Surprising though it might be, there is a real sense in which Wheatley brought philosophy to the story of the occult. It is also true that he brought sadism, chauvinism, racism, sexism, flagellation, and stocking tops, some of which might have been present implicitly before, but never as the raison d'être of the story.

Most of these other contributions of Dennis Wheatley are present in *To the Devil – A Daughter*, which is customarily linked with *The Devil Rides Out* and *The Haunting of Toby Jugg* as one of his major stories of the occult. The story concerns a plot by the Russians to take over the world by creating an army of homunculi by complex occult processes involving a considerable expenditure of maidens; the hero refers to his mother throughout as 'Mumsie'; and Wheatley's description of the various physical assaults made upon the heroine have secured for him the distinction of having published a book in 1964 that is still expurgated in most of its published forms in 1978. There is none of the philosophizing that gave an added dimension to *The Haunting of Toby Jugg* and at least an unexpected interest to *Strange Conflict* and *The Devil Rides Out*; and the level of general discussion is indicated by remarks such as: 'The best example I can give you of an ace-high Black Magician in modern times is the monk Rasputin. He did more than all the Bolsheviks put together to bring about the Russian revolution; and I don't need to tell you the extent of the evil that has brought to Russia, and may yet bring to the rest of the world.' As always with Dennis Wheatley, the question of erotic symbolism does not arise: instead we are treated to scientifically-observed descriptions of the heroine's thighs which read like extracts from a treatise on applied mechanics: '"Just feel, here by my suspenders." Suddenly taking his hand, she pulled it forward till it touched the inner side of her thigh on a line with the top of her other stocking. The flesh there was like a cushion of swansdown under a taut-stretched skin of tissue-thin rubber; it had that indefinable quality of being cool at first touch, then instantly radiating heat.'

The enigma of Dennis Wheatley is obviously going to remain unsolved. There is no discernible line of development in his fiction, except for a growing explicitness in titillating descriptions in line with the relaxation of literary conventions in this area, and he is not likely to resolve any contradictions at the age of eighty. He brought to occult fiction incomparable gifts for the creation of incident, for the exposition of a coherent philosophy of the occult, and for the development of narrative. They were accompanied by other qualities and values which would normally be fatal to any creative effort whatever. It is the measure of Wheatley's failure to reconcile his inconsistencies that after writing for over forty years on the general theme of mankind's struggle with the Devil, his readers should have reason to doubt whether he actually thinks there is a Devil or not, or even which side he really is on.[4]

Notes

1 *The Lure of the Occult*

1. There is always a real problem of definition here. Terms like 'supernatural' are not really satisfactory, because obviously anything that can be experienced in any form at all must exist in nature, and therefore, deserves to be categorized as natural. Experiences can be unusual, uncomfortable or undesirable, but they cannot be unnatural. 'Paranormal' may well be the most logical and generally satisfactory term for phenomena beyond the bounds of the physical universe, but it may still be too technical-sounding to be completely acceptable. 'Occult' which is used almost throughout here, is both familiar and also exact, strictly speaking: paranormal phenomena cannot be unnatural if they exist, but they are certainly 'hidden' from us in the sense that they cannot be analyzed experimentally or theorized about rigorously the way that normal physical phenomena can. This is of course what makes them paranormal.

2. Some writers in this field have developed almost to the point of art the technique of deploying alleged data which sounds impressive, but which is in fact literally

meaningless. The classic example is perhaps Bram Stoker himself, in *The Lady of the Shroud*, where his seven foot tall hero consoles himself for the problems that might lie ahead if his lady-love should prove to be a vampire by thinking of tough spots that he has been in in the past. He thinks of 'wild mystic rites held in the deep gloom of African forests. when, amid scenes of revolting horror, Obi and the devils of his kind, seemed to reveal themselves to reckless worshippers, surfeited with horror, whose lives counted for naught; when even human sacrifice was an episode, and the reek of old devilries and recent carnage tainted the air, till even I, who was, at the risk of my life, a privileged spectator, who had come through dangers without end to behold the scene, rose and fled in horror. Of scenes of mystery enacted in rock-cut temples beyond the Himalayas, whose fanatic priests, cold as death and as remorseless, in the reaction of their frenzy of passion, foamed at the mouth and then sank into marble quiet, as with inner eyes they beheld the visions of the hellish powers which they had evoked. Of wild, fantastic dances of the Devil-worshippers of Madagascar, where even the very semblance of humanity disappeared in the fantastic excesses of their orgies. Of strange doings of gloom and mystery in the rock-parched monasteries of Tibet. Of awful sacrifices, all to mystic ends, in the innermost recesses of Cathay.... Of rites of most inconceivable horror in the fastnesses of Patagonia, etc, etc.' Stoker gives no real indication what was going on at any stage of these performances, and presumably had no idea himself. However he could rely on the imagination of the reader to elaborate endlessly on the general themes of strange doings and inconceivable horrors.

3. Howard P. Lovecraft, 'Supernatural Horror in Literature', in *Dagon and Other Macabre Tales* (London 1969), p. 143.

4. Among the most important and influential studies published or reprinted recently would be: E. Y. Evans-Wentz, *Bardo Thodol: The Tibetan Book of the Dead* (New York 1960); C. G. Jung, *Synchronicity* (London 1972); Arthur Koestler, *The Roots of Coincidence* (London 1972), and *Life After Death* (London 1976); E. Kubler-Ross, *Death: The Final Stage of Growth* (Englewood Cliffs 1975); and Raymond L. Moody, *Life After Life* (Atlanta 1975), and *Reflection on Life After Life* (Atlanta 1977). There is certainly abundant evidence that the age in which science has begun the exploration of outer space is also the age in which interest in the occult has been more widespread and overt than it has been for at least three hundred years. For example, a poll conducted by the *New Scientist* in 1972 revealed that nearly seventy percent of the respondents, most of whom were scientists or technicians, believed in the possibility of extra-sensory perception. A public opinion poll taken in Australia towards the end of 1974 discovered that twenty-nine percent of the population believed in some kind of personal devil, and eighteen percent believed in evil spirits. This may indeed understate the real position: the director of a youth aid organization in Sydney, New South Wales, claimed in August 1975 that one hundred percent of students in some Sydney schools were involved with the occult, their interests ranging from ' experimentation with ouija boards and tarot fortune telling cards to satanic sex rites of black masses and mind domination'; and the Queensland director of the same organization testified that about twelve percent of senior high school students in that state were involved with the occult, warned parents to be alert to 'knocking sounds in the home, sudden dropping of a room's temperature from comfortable to chilly, and a general depression and unsociability'. Anglican Church inquiry commissions found

that half of the high school students in Sydney, Brisbane and Adelaide had dealings with the occult, believed in Satan, and 'played at' contacting spirits. It cannot seriously be suggested that many people reading stories of the occult in the seventies of this century are doing so to reinforce their own rational disbelief in such phenomena. More people are reading occult fiction than ever before, because more people than ever before are prepared to believe that it might be to some extent fiction based upon fact. There are indeed no limits now to our readiness to consider as worthy of serious investigation alleged phenomena which have literally never been taken seriously before. The agricultural and horticultural experiments carried out at Findhorn Bay Caravan Park, Forrest, Scotland, have reaffirmed belief in wood-sprites, barghests, elves, kelpies and assorted fairies. This would seem to provide quite a new dimension to our comprehension of the occult: if we are to believe in fairies, there is really nothing left to disbelieve in. (See William I. Thompson, *Passages about Earth* (New York 1974), for a scholarly and scientific examination of the Findhorn experiments).

2 *Vampires and Ladies*

1. Lovecraft, *Supernatural Horror in Literature*, p. 167.
2. Among the works of Dickens examples include Edith Granger and Florence Dombey, in *Dombey and Son*; Bella Wilfer and Lizzie Hexham in *Our Mutual Friend*; Esther Summerson and Ada Clare in *Bleak House*; and most fervent and emotionally developed, Helena Landless and Rosa Budd in *Edwin Drood*; and among those of Meredith, the scenes between Diana Merion and Emma in *Diana of the Crossways*; the Countess de Saladar and Mrs Strike in *Evan Harrington*; and Vittoria and Giacinta in *Vittoria*, where the

E

latter becomes the first woman to have her breast kissed in respectable English fiction since Sophia Western's painful experience in *Tom Jones*. Sophia of course has her breast kissed by a man; Giacinta, by another woman. What was acceptable to the eighteenth century was not always acceptable to the nineteenth century, and the reverse may well have been true in some cases. The basic incongruity of the Victorian convention in literature is indicated by the fact that Dickens and Meredith among others found themselves far less constrained when describing passionate verbal and physical exchanges between women, than they would have been in the case of depicting such exchanges between persons of different sexes. The quality of homosexual emotions is thus customarily more intense and more convincing in their novels than that of heterosexual ones. We may presume that this was not the original idea.

3 *Sex and Horror*

1. Lovecraft, *Supernatural Horror in Literature*, p. 196.
2. Stoker is obviously a most improbable writer of the occult, and it might certainly be assumed that he came to write such books of the occult at all only because of a psychological compulsion to exorcize the demons of guilt and repression inflicted on him by Florence. Married to almost anybody else, Stoker would in all likelihood have confined himself to tales of high adventure, for which indeed he showed a genuine ability. *The Lady of the Shroud*, which is by far his happiest book, is a straightforward Ruritanian romance, with characters larger than life, plenty of effective local colour and an enthusiastic parade of military technology which anticipates James Bond: at one stage the gigantic hero, who is also a millionaire, orders a 'torpedo yacht ... built by Thorneycroft, engined by Parsons, armoured by

Armstrong, armed by Crupp; three suits of Masterman bullet-proof clothes', and even an aircraft, 'a Kitson', which seemed to have all the useful characteristics of airship and helicopter, as well of course as 'fifty thousand of the newest-pattern rifles, the French Inglis-Malbron, which has surpassed all others'. Stoker's credentials as a spiritual ancestor of James Bond are reinforced by the fact that the heroine of *The Lady of the Shroud* is perhaps the first white heroine in English fiction to take off her clothes in a man's bedroom, with the man still actually present. She admittedly disrobes behind a screen, but Stoker provides helpful sound effects. 'She bowed gravely, and taking the dressing gown in a long, white, finely-shaped hand, bore it behind the screen. There was a slight rustle, and then a hollow 'flop' as the wet garment fell on the floor'. It is a world away from the steaming symbolism of *Dracula*.

3. Leonard Wolf, *The Annotated Dracula* (New York 1975), p. 3.

4. Fair is fair, and a case for the defence has been made out for the vampire, whether one finds it convincing or not. In a letter to *Time Magazine*, 13 June 1977, Mr Donald A. Reed, President of the Count Dracula Society, Los Angeles, argues that: 'Dracula is much more than a mere historical hero. Dracula stands as the symbol and essence of philosophies of the East and the West. Dracula presents the messages of resurrection, transmigration, rebirth, renewal and immortality. Our love of horror films and gothic literature brought us to Dracula and the founding of this national nonprofit society sixteen years ago. But we, of course, have long realized Dracula's symbolic importance in our culture.'

4 *Love after Death*

1. Lilias Rider Haggard, *The Cloak That I left* (London 1951), p. 276.
2. Lilias Rider Haggard, *Cloak*, p. 20. Haggard never abdicated his judgement: he was consistent in attitude, although never exactly so in language. There is a sense in which Haggard could quite correctly be termed an agnostic, in that he rigorously resisted any temptation to define the indefinable. The nearest he ever came to an unqualified statement of belief may be in the opening page of a didactic and generally dreary novel, *Love Eternal*: 'More than 30 years ago two atoms of the eternal Energy sped forth from the heart of it which we call God, and incarnated themselves in the human shapes that were destined to hold them for a while, as vases hold perfumes, goblets wine or as specks of everlasting radium inhabit the bowels of the rock. Perhaps these two atoms, or essences, or monads indestructible, did but repeat an adventure, or many, many adventures.... If so, over what fields did they roam through the aeons, they who having no end, could have no beginning. Not those of this world only, we may be sure.' The indispensable word is 'perhaps'. Haggard did not believe in final answers. Nor does he seem to be really interested in the attempts of his characters to find final answers: his alter ego, *Allan Quatermain*, describes in *She and Allan* how in his search for reassurance about life after death he 'met a man who was a spiritualist to whom I confided a little of my perplexities. He laughed at me and said that they could be settled with the greatest of ease. All I had to do was to visit a certain medium who for a fee of one guinea would tell me everything I wanted to know. Although I rather grudged the guinea, being more than usually hard up at the time, I called upon this person, but over the

results of that visit, or rather the lack of them, I draw a veil. My queer and perhaps unwholesome longing, however, remained with me and would not be abated. I consulted a clergyman of my acquaintance, a good and spiritually-minded man, but he could only shrug his shoulders and refer me to the Bible, saying, quite rightly I doubt not, that with what it reveals I ought to be contented. Then I read certain mystical books that were recommended to me. These were full of fine words, undiscoverable in a pocket dictionary, but really took me no forwarder, since in them I found nothing I could not have invented myself ... I even tackled Swedenborg, or rather samples of him, for he is very copious, but without satisfactory results. Then I gave up the business'. In fact he consults an old witchdoctor, in whom he pretends not to believe, and is sent by him to meet Ayesha, whom he does not know what to make of. Haggard's message would seem to be that this side of the grave one can learn of the occult neither from one's own experience nor from that of others.

3. Lilias Rider Haggard, *Cloak*, p. 260.
4. Lilias Rider Haggard, *Cloak*, p. 129.

5 *The Myth that Never was*

1. L. Sprague de Camp, *Lovecraft: a Biography* (New York 1974) pp. 30–31, 52.
2. de Camp, *Lovecraft*, p. 194.
3. Architecture seems to have been one of Lovecraft's more comprehensible passions, to which he responded with a characteristic lack of any kind of restraint: in a quite irrelevant passage in the same story, he refers to 'the Fleur-de-Lys building in Thomas Street, a hideous Victorian imitation of seventeenth-century Breton architecture which flaunts its stuccoed front amidst the lovely Colonial houses on the ancient hill, and under

the very shadow of the finest Georgian steeple in America.' Lovecraft's adoration of the classical style in architecture as in prose style is yet another of the anomalies inherent in his psychological condition: nobody could have closer affinities with the nineteenth-century Gothic or fewer with eighteenth or seventeenth century classicism than Lovecraft himself, in his life as in his work. He abhors the style of which he was himself the most thorough-going exemplar, and adores the one every principle of which his own manner would have offended against.

4. de Camp, ' H. P. Lovecraft: Master of Fantasy ', *Dialogue*, 8 (1975), pp. 109–116.

5. de Camp, *Lovecraft,* p. 31.

6. Vincent Buranelli, *Edgar Allan Poe* (New York 1961), p. 62. Buranelli goes on to argue that Poe has ' a strong claim to the titles of our best poet, our best short story writer, and our best critic ', and that he is indeed ' America's greatest writer, and the American writer of greatest significance in world literature '. Even Lovecraft's most unconditional admirers might hesitate before going that far in their admiration for the creator of Cthulhu.

6 *Orthodox Horrors*

1. There have been other attempts by writers to cash in on Blatty's success, however: we have so far had *The Omen, The Sentinel, The Other,* and in cinema *The Heretic* (*Exorcist* II), which could most appropriately have been entitled *The Return of Puzazu.*

7 *The Devil and Dennis Wheatley*

1. For Wheatley's views on Charles II, a subject for whom he has considerable sympathy, see *Old Rowley* (London

1933); for his account of the Russian Revolution, on which he has at least strong feelings, see *Red Eagle* (London 1937); and *Stranger than Fiction* (London 1959), an extremely interesting record of his own experiences as a member of the Joint Planning Staff in the Second World War. The first volume of his memoirs is *The Young Man Said, 1897–1914* (London 1977).

2. One can only be impressed by the fact that rape is actually the normal form of relationship between the sexes in Wheatley's stories. The hero of *The Man Who Missed the War* seduces the heroine after helping her to get drunk, while Roger Brook, the rapist and torturer of Russian princesses, rapes his cousin Georgina, who has already received her sexual initiation by being raped by a highwayman in *The Launching of Roger Brook*. Sally Cardew in *The Haunting of Toby Jugg* and Christina in *To the Devil – a Daughter* are prepared or scheduled for rape, even though the actual assault is not carried out. The epileptic hero of *Mayhem in Greece*, whom Mr Wheatley portrays as a vulgar half-wit, rapes the very sympathetic heroine. There is no suggestion that the women involved have any serious grounds for resenting their treatment.

3. Stocking tops were undoubtedly the most popular sexual fetish of the pre-pantyhose generation, and no writer not overtly dealing in pornography ever got more mileage out of stocking tops than Dennis Wheatley. The curious reader is referred in particular to *Come Into My Parlour* (stocking tops, murder, Nazis and sadism); *Star of Ill-Omen* (stocking tops, adultery, Communists and flying saucers); *Curtain of Fear* (stocking tops, Communists and flagellation); and especially *To The Devil – A Daughter* (stocking tops, Communists and the production of homunculi).

4. The incongruity of Dennis Wheatley's having as a hero a devil-figure who is even satanic in appearance has

already been mentioned. But there is nothing more certain than that Wheatley does not know what he thinks about the Devil, despite the fact that the latter has played the dominant part in his writings for over forty years. It is remarkable enough that a book entitled *The Devil Rides Out* should contain a passage like: 'There is no such person as the Devil, but there are vast numbers of Earthbound spirits, Elementals and Evil Intelligences of the Outer Circle floating in our midst.' But fourteen years later, Toby Jugg is even more confused. Having reflected that 'while it remains an open question whether any human being has ever seen the Devil, it seems impossible to doubt the existence of demons', he then goes on to assert that 'the general decline of religion since the end of the Victorian era has enormously facilitated the Devil's age-old task of replacing order by chaos, and at last, entering into his Principality of this world as the Lord of Misrule'. As always Wheatley seems quite unaware of any lack of order in his own ideas.

Bibliography

Browne, Nelson, *Sheridan Le Fanu* (London 1951)

Cohen, Morton N., *Rider Haggard: His Life and Work* (London 1968)

Cohen, Morton N., *Rudyard Kipling to Rider: The Record of a Friendship* (London 1965)

Derleth, August (ed.), *H. P. Lovecraft and Others: Tales of the Cthulhu Mythos* vols I and II (London 1975)

Farson, Daniel, *The Man Who Wrote Dracula* (London 1976)

Greene, Grahame, 'Rider Haggard's Secret', *Collected Essays* (New York 1969)

Hadfield, A. M., *An Introduction to Charles Williams* (London 1959)

Heath-Stubbs, John, *Charles Williams* (London 1952)

Masters, Alfred, *The Natural History of the Vampire* (London 1972)

Miller, Henry, *Books in My Life* (London 1951)

Osborne, Charles, *The Bram Stoker Bedside Companion* (London 1973)

Parry, Michael, *The Rivals of Dracula* (London 1977)

Penzoldt, Peter, *The Supernatural in Fiction* (New York 1965)

Rider Haggard, Henry, *The Days of My Life* (London 1926)

Ronay, Gabriel, *The Dracula Myth* (New York 1972)

Wolf, Leonard, *A Dream of Dracula* (Boston 1972)

Wilson, Colin, *The Strength to Dream* (London 1962)

Index